GREAT WALKS
SCOTLAND

GREAT WALKS

SCOTLAND

HAMISH BROWN, RENNIE McOWAN & RICHARD MEARNS
Photography by John Heseltine

With an Introduction by JIMMIE MacGREGOR

Series Editor Frank Duerden

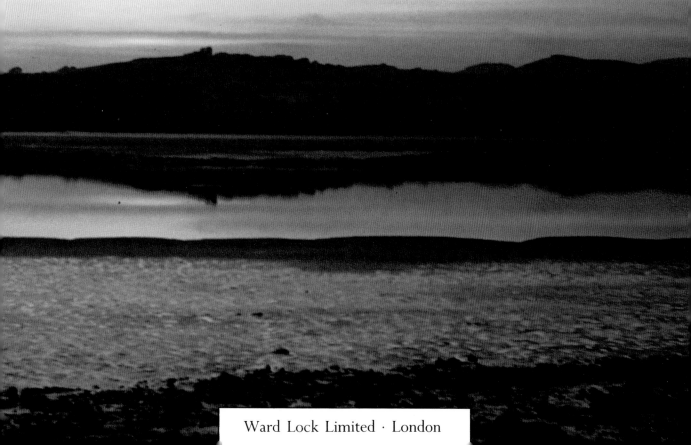

Ward Lock Limited · London

© Text Richard Mearns, Rennie McOwan, Hamish Brown, 1989, 1991
© Photography Ward Lock Limited 1989, 1991
Map artwork by Peter Bull Art

First published in Great Britain in 1989
by Ward Lock Limited, Villiers House,
41–47 Strand, London WC2N 5JE
a Cassell Company

First paperback edition 1991

Text filmset in Perpetua
by M & R Computerised Typesetting Ltd, of Grimsby, South Humberside

Printed and bound in Singapore

British Library Cataloguing in Publication Data
Brown, Hamish M. *1934–*
  Scotland — (Great Walks).
  1. Scotland. Recreations: Walking —
  Visitors' guides
  I. Title II. McOwan, Rennie
  III. Mearns, Richard IV. Series
796.5′1′09411

    ISBN 0-7063-70554 paperback
    ISBN 0-7063-6749-9

Half title page: *The island of Mull*
Title page: *The Solway Firth*

CONTENTS

INTRODUCTION

As a boy, the highest place in my world was the flagpole mound in Glasgow's Springburn park, and the wildest places I knew were the streets of the city. My secret hidden places were the stair wells, dunnies and back courts of the tenements, and my cliffs were four stories of sandstone. Springburn stands high in Glasgow, and from the viewpoint of the park there were grand, and seemingly remote vistas to the north. Between the canyons of the high buildings which packaged the poor, there were glimpses of another bigger and emptier world. A world of blurred blue hills, and mysteriously, glints of snow in spring sunshine. As I grew, I was drawn to these places. The hills were the Campsies, a mere 11 miles distant, and the unseasonal snow gleamed on Ben Lomond at only twice that distance. The bicycle made the Campsies accessible, and a great physical day began with the cycle ride to Campsie Glen. The bike would then be hidden, so that I could climb to the summit ridge and wander miles of open moor, tracking down the nests of peewit, curlew and wheatear. Once, on the loose rock, there was the thrill of a kestrel's nest with five russet eggs. On descending from the hill, one could cool off in the icy waters that ran through the glen before pedalling home. Through walking, cycling and cross-country running, (we hadn't heard of jogging) I became familiar with the countryside around where I then lived, on the edge of the town. I was fascinated by the wildlife, and the more I learned, the more I wanted to know.

I was moving farther afield now, and in my teenage years I was already familiar with what is now known as the West Highland Way. I discovered the Scottish Youth Hostels, and made good use of all those close to Glasgow, as well as some further afield: Fintry, Inverbeg, Crianlarich, Glencoe, The Isle of Arran, (a favourite place) Rowerdennan, Ardgarten and Auchendennan. Later, when a student, I worked at Auchen-dennan as an assistant warden; and much later as an art teacher, I introduced scores of youngsters to the outdoors by walking them over the hills from Campsie Glen to Fintry Youth Hostel.

When I became embroiled in the world of folk music, skiffle and jazz in London, the outdoors played a diminished part in my life for some years, although Hampstead Heath was always there for walking and running, and concert tours abroad provided some off-beat opportunities, like blistering hill walks in Israel.

When touring in Scotland's highlands and islands, I found it useful to have a pair of boots in the car, for there were opportunities for walks between concert venues. I still remember the thrill of finding my first ring ouzel's nest, on a little walk on stolen time between Brora and Inverness.

The direction of my life and career has changed once again, and I now find myself privileged to be making radio and television programmes all over Scotland, and it is strange to reflect that all my youthful obsessions which were considered odd, if not downright eccentric, have now become commonplace. Any library or good bookshop now has a section devoted to outdoor pursuits, and manufacturers of boots, outdoor clothing and climbing gear emerge from their Porsches wearing beatific smiles.

The increase in the number of people taking to the hills and wild places carries its own dangers of course, but on balance, it can only be a good thing that more and more people are enjoying Scotland's countryside and wilderness areas, and, most importantly, caring for them. *Great Walks of Scotland* can only add to the interest in, and concern for, the country. The three authors of this book are all vastly experienced outdoor people, who combine knowledge with real concern for what has shaped Scotland's landscape and country life in the past, what is happening now, and what could take place in the future.

Rennie McOwan's name is known to anyone interested in Scotland, and in addition to his numerous writings, he does regular broadcasts, and has even helped me out on my own radio and television programmes. Despite the fact that Rennie deplores the concept of marked walk-ways, and I make programmes about them, we remain friends, and I have a deep respect for his knowledge of Scottish life, including history, ornithology and the arts. Although Rennie McOwan is a very busy writer, lecturer and broadcaster, he still spends as much time as possible on the hills, and is descended from a long line of outdoor people. His grandfather and great-grandfather were well-known stalkers on the Langwell and Braemore estate in Caithness, and feature prominently in the memoirs of the Laird, the Duke of Portland.

Hamish Brown is one of Scotland's best-known outdoor men, with eleven books and countless newspaper and magazine articles to his credit. He shares Rennie McOwan's interest in ornithology, music and the arts, and while he is very much associated with Scotland, he was brought up in the Far East, and has travelled extensively in places as diverse as Morocco, Ethiopia, Iceland, Poland, Corsica and the Pyrenees.

Richard Mearns has made a special study of the lives of early

Scottish ornithologists, and like our other two authors, has travelled widely. Richard is employed as a senior countryside ranger on the western section of the Southern Upland Way, and is especially attracted to walks in the south of Scotland. In addition to his other writings, he has undertaken scientific publications on the raven and the peregrine falcon.

In *Great Walks of Scotland*, our three writers have given us a huge range and variety of routes, together with enough densely textured background information to keep most outdoor enthusiasts interested and challenged for a long time to come. Interesting as they may all be to read, their common object is to persuade you to lace up your boots and venture forth to find out about this wonderful country for yourself.

Jimmie Macgregor

THE FACE OF SCOTLAND

Rennie McOwan

There are more spectacular and far higher mountains in many other lands, but perhaps Scotland has two factors which make its hill country almost unique. The first is weather and changing light. We can wince at the amount of rain and mutter inwardly as we bow our heads to hail and sleet. There can be many weeks of dark and dank weather, but it does mean that a particular view, a hill or mountain range is rarely the same and that temperatures change. One day the hills are grape-blue, the next black, green or grey. They can look far away or close up, they swim in and out of hail and rain storms, and change in cloud shadow. They shine with new snow or shimmer in days of sun. The weather is changeable and the mountains change with it: their shape, outline, effect and, above all, their colours.

The second factor is that of changing character in relation to size. Scotland is slightly smaller than, say, England, yet, unlike some other much larger countries, it does not have one face. Within a few miles a traveller can move from coastal fishing villages and fertile fields to upland moors and farms and then to higher hills. The mainland mass can be traversed by car in a day and the traveller can pass from lonely mountains to the industrial heartland, from large, prairie-like fields to lochs, woods and moors, and sometimes within one area. Occasionally this quick-change act can be startling and yet it is one of the attractions of Scotland. Within the whole, its hills and mountains also change in character, from the rocky peaks of the north and north-west to the softer hills of the southern Highlands and the Borders, from the mountains of the west, split by lonely lochs and passes, to the plateau-like Cairngorms or the hills of the islands which are navigation markers for sailors. There is an immense variety of terrain and territory, of appeal and interest, that no one can exhaust in a lifetime.

Although the hills are relatively small, they are not to be taken lightly and have produced many mountaineers of world calibre. As early as the nineteenth century some of the first formal climbers appreciated that Scottish snow and ice were excellent training for the Alps and some have argued, then and since, that the spring and winter scene at home was equally demanding and often more rewarding than that abroad.

Scotland is often referred to as a small country and that is true in terms of its population of only five million. There are immense advantages in a low population density when it comes to enjoying the amount of available wild land or, to be precise, the amount of land where the hand of man is least evident, and there are obvious consequent benefits for 'stravaiging' (wandering), hill walking or general rambling.

Access is dealt with on pages 171–2, but this combination of much wild land and a relatively small population, of whom over half are concentrated in the industrialized or agriculture-intensive central belt, tends to mean that there are relatively few access problems and that tension-points or instances of harmful pressure of visitors on beauty spots are few.

There is an immense richness in Scottish wild life and in botanical life, and these, too, change with the seasons. Happy the person who can add an interest in birds and animals, flowers and plants, geology and social history to their overall love of being on hill ground and of walking the summits and passes.

Geologically, Scotland is a complex country and much pioneer research was conducted by Scots and is reflected in the use of Scottish placenames for rocks, such as Lewisian gneiss (named after the island of Lewis, in the Outer Hebrides). Almost 3,000 million years old, gneiss is a complex of the most ancient rock types in Britain and one of the oldest in the world, and is prominent in the north-west Highlands and the Outer Hebrides.

THE MOUNTAIN AREAS

Traditionally, people tend to divide Scotland, like Gaul, into three parts—the Highlands, the Central Lowlands and the Southern Uplands—but for walking and mountaineering purposes further subdivision is often necessary to truly appreciate the changing character of the hills.

In the far north lie the spectacular peaks of Assynt and other parts of Sutherland, *suderland*, the 'south land' of the Norsemen, and Wester Ross has its fine mountains too. The flat lands of Caithness are dominated to the south by the prominent peak of Morven, literally 'the big mountain', and the start of hill ground. In the north, too, are castle-like Stac Polly, rocky Suilven, the many peaks of Quinag, and several others. There are splendid viewpoint hills like northerly Ben Hope, or Ben More Assynt and its neighbour, Conival, shapely Ben Loyal at Tongue, or grassy Ben Wyvis in Easter Ross.

The northern section also includes the striking hills of Torridon, Beinn Alligin, soaring Liathach, grey Beinn Eighe, magnificent Slioch above Loch Maree, the lonely peaks behind Slioch in one of the last wildernesses, and the sharp outline of An Teallach, above Little Loch Broom.

Here is a land mainly composed of moorland, stones, lonely lochans and peaks like the remaining teeth in the abandoned skull of a deer or sheep.

In the Western Highlands are other glens and hills, which can only be reached by plodding many miles, and many large mountains of character, not so rocky as some of the northern peaks, but dominating and impressive. Here are hills like Ladhar Bheinn, in lonely Knoydart, now in the care of the John Muir Trust, a new conservation body named after Dunbar-born John Muir, the father of American conservation. Here, too, are the hills around Loch Arkaig and Glen Dessary, with the memories of the fugitive Prince Charles Edward Stuart, the many tops of the Cluanie Ridge, the notched Saddle which overlooks Glen Shiel, the Five Sisters of Kintail, the Glen Affric and Strathfarrar hills. It is a land often split on the west by fiord-like sea lochs.

The Central Highlands change yet again, dominated by Ben Nevis, the highest mountain in Britain, a mixture of huge hills and ranges, sections of which attract enthusiasts of technical rock, snow and ice climbing, the Glen Coe hills, Nevis itself and its huge cliffs, the linking summits of the Mamores, twin-topped Ben Cruachan in Argyll, the Blackmount peaks, the hills fringing Rannoch Moor. Then there is the plateau-mound of Ben Alder, where the hunted Jacobite chief, Cluny MacPherson, hid out for many years, the rounded hills at Drumochter fringing the busy A9, Creag Meaghaidh, near Laggan, popular with winter climbers, and the pleasant plateau of the Monadh Liath, near Newtonmore, an ancient hill name ('grey moors') still on our modern maps.

The Cairngorms, of course, are mainly a huge plateau and the popular peaks, Cairngorm itself, Cairn Toul, Braeriach, Ben MacDhui (second only to Nevis in height), Ben Avon and Beinn a' Bhuird, make them one of the great mountain ranges and, again, with a variable character. They contain rocky and spectacular sections but although they are mainly rounded hills they are not to be trifled with: weather can be fierce and distances great. The beautiful hills of Glen Tilt, in Perthshire, Beinn a'Ghlo and its neighbours, royal Lochnagar on Deeside, and the striking passes of the Lairig Ghru, Glen Feshie, Lairig an Laoigh, the Minigaig, Gaick and the Tolmount (Jock's Road) passes, also fall within the general Cairngorms definition. It also includes Strath Spey, parts of Moray, Angus, lower Deeside, the

Echoes of the past on Skye

Mearns and Don and Deveronside.

The Southern Highlands are softer, their straths more fertile, and yet they also have their rocky peaks and lonely corners. The three-topped Cobbler, at Arrochar, on Loch Long, is a favourite peak with rock climbers, Ben Lomond is ascended by thousands of visitors each year, the Trossachs peaks are also busy, Ben Lui at Tyndrum and its prominent corrie draws the spring and winter climbers, and the summits of the Crianlarich hills, of Mamlorn, the Killin hills, and the area around Glen Lyon attract many hill trampers. This grouping also includes Ben Lawers, near Killin, Perthshire, famed for its Alpine flora, and cone-shaped Schiehallion, at Loch Rannoch. The lower ranges near the big industrial cities, the Kilpatricks and Campsies, near Glasgow, also come into this section, as do the central Ochils and Fife Lomonds.

The Southern Uplands contain the rounded hills of the Borders and Ayrshire, Edinburgh's Pentland Hills, the rougher hills of Galloway, which can look like the Highlands in miniature and which include the Merrick, at 2,764 ft (842 m) the highest hill on the Scottish mainland south of the Highland line, and many other grassy corners, a mixture of moorland and hill farms, lovely rivers, tucked-away little towns and much modern conifer forestry.

The last general grouping is the islands, the peerless Cuillin of Skye, the smaller Cuillin of Rhum, the big hills of Harris in the Outer Hebrides, the holiday island of Arran with its spectacular hills, Mull of the cool, high bens, as the Gaelic song has it, and many another green and golden gem in blue and jade seas.

THE GAELIC PRESENCE

It is perhaps the Gaelic-speaking people, the descendants of the older Celtic races, who have left the major mark on Scotland's hill landscape. Gaelic was once spoken in most of the Highland areas and also in Galloway, in the south-west, and lingers on in parts of Scotland yet. It existed in some Lowland areas alongside a kind of Welsh or Brittonic, the language of the Britons of Strathclyde and the Picts, and the Scots language itself. Later a kind of Norman French entered Scottish court language and intermingled with the Scots language. Some Scottish hill names in Lowland areas, such as the Ochils, include names which are Gaelic, Brittonic, Lowland Scots and modern English or a mixture of all. In the north and west, Gaelic and Norse or Old Norse names are intermingled.

Another sign the Gaelic people left for us in more modern

centuries was the drove roads through the hills, the routes cattle took from the Highlands and Islands to the great fairs at Crieff or Falkirk and in the north of England. Cattle reiving (stealing) in past times was thought to be more of a manly sport than a crime, but by the eighteenth century cattle-rearing and selling had evolved into big business. By the time of the Napoleonic wars thousands of beasts went south to meet the demand for meat from the Army and Navy and later from the increasingly urbanized populations of the Industrial Revolution. These drove routes go through many of the main passes and their rest stances, grassy, flat areas, can still be seen, although some are vanishing under private conifer forestry. The use of these routes petered out in the late nineteenth century when agricultural practices changed and transport improved.

THE CHANGING HIGHLANDS

When the eighteenth-century Jacobite Risings failed and the power of the chiefs was curbed, Highland landscape was to alter, and particularly so in the following century. Some pioneering agricultural or forestry work had begun, crofting developed, small and often short-lived industries such as kelp collecting and burning were instituted and, most dramatic of all, the sheep came from the Lowlands and Borders in large numbers and the big sporting estates were created.

At one time the chief and his family held the land on behalf of everybody and clanspeople had a real dignity and a strong feeling of equality. Then a more feudal structure came which, in turn, had changed by the nineteenth century to landowning on a pattern similar to that of a modern estate and often with non-Highland owners. The former clan unity gave way to the relationship of landlord and tenant.

Many Highlanders emigrated, some willingly, many forced to leave in what became known as the Clearances. It is a sad and controversial story. The remains of their townships from the days of the earlier cattle economy and post-clan days can be seen in the glens and straths, and some Highland glens which once held many families now hold one farm or house or none at all. Sheep were more profitable than people, but in time sheep, too, failed to pay and were replaced on many estates by deer.

The remains of military roads can also be seen in many parts of the hill land and particularly in the Highlands, grassy or heather-overgrown tracks often running alongside the modern roads and through strategic passes, and some replaced drove-road tracks. Many modern roads follow the line of the military roads and so do some of the others constructed and surveyed by the great engineer Thomas Telford (1757–1834) who was the chief engineer on the Caledonian Canal, and engineer to the Commissioners for Highland Roads and Bridges from 1803.

The Victorian railway engineers also followed many of Telford's research lines and in some glens or straths one can see a modern road, a railway, the remains of an old military road and a drove road running alongside one another.

New maps, new roads and railways, and new demands for development, also helped change the face of the hills. The railways opened them up to mountaineers and walkers from distant areas. By Victorian times thousands of navvies from Scotland and England, and even more from Ireland, laboured to make roads, dams, reservoirs and canals and later constructed the twentieth-century hydro-electric schemes.

The coming of the sheep and the birth of the big, sporting estates in the nineteenth century changed the face of much of the Highland landscape. The sheep is a devouring monster and by preventing regeneration it removed miles of woodland from lower hillsides and glens which once had a covering of pine, alder, birch, hazel and juniper. The old Caledonian pine forests had also vanished over the centuries as they were felled and fired to flush out fugitives, to provide timber for houses or shipping, or burned for industrial purposes. Oak woods in southern areas were 'managed' so as to obtain the bark used in the tanning of leather, and much woodland was burned for charcoal to be used in the smelting of iron ore.

Many animal species died out: the elk, beaver, wild boar, brown bear, lynx and the wolf. Some are commemorated in hill names such as Ben Oss, at Tyndrum, Perthshire, 'mountain of the elk'.

Old Highland records speak of people being able to walk from Gairloch on the west coast to Dornoch on the east coast and never be totally out of woodland. Although royal deer forests in medieval centuries were closely administered and deer poaching severely punished, nevertheless people roamed freely, naturally and of right, in their own hills and glens. The big nineteenth-century sheep farms and deer-sporting estates curtailed this for the first time. Because some travel was obviously necessary between communities, for trade, to market, school, or on coffin routes, legislation created rights-of-way, corridor-walking through glens and passes which had legal protection. The pattern of social life in many of these glens and communities has now gone forever and so have the people, but the corridor routes retain their protected status. It must be said that while freedom-to-roam in Scotland has a long pedigree, the

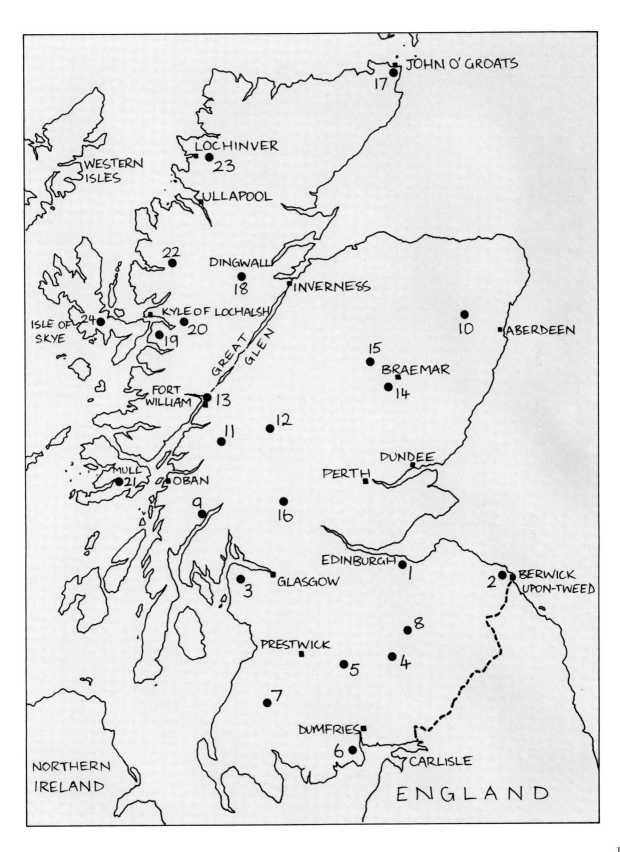

JOHN O'GROATS
17

LOCHINVER
23

WESTERN
ISLES

ULLAPOOL

22

DINGWALL

18

INVERNESS

ISLE OF
SKYE

24

KYLE OF LOCHALSH
20

19

10 ABERDEEN

15

BRAEMAR
14

GREAT GLEN

FORT
WILLIAM 13

11

12

DUNDEE

PERTH

MULL
21

OBAN

9

16

EDINBURGH
1

BERWICK
UPON-TWEED
2

GLASGOW
3

8

PRESTWICK

5

4

7

DUMFRIES

6

CARLISLE

NORTHERN
IRELAND

E N G L A N D

creation of rights-of-way is a controversial subject. Rights-of-way are not given on Ordnance Survey maps of Scotland.

Edwardian and Victorian aristocrats and industrialists holidayed on the northern estates in a mixture of outdoor romanticism and practical sport. The numbers of red deer rose as herds were increased and managed and today they, too, play a significant part in preventing woodland regenerating. Sporting estates and the commercial sale of venison are still an integral part of Highland life.

EARLY MOUNTAINEERING

Many mountaineering books record eighteenth- and nineteenth-century travellers as being among the first hillwalkers in Scotland, but this is to totally ignore the native Gaelic or Celtic peoples. They were truly the first mountaineers, both as cragsmen and hill trampers, but when mountaineering developed as a recreational sport, often with scientific or natural history overtones, many Scots were prominent in the development of Scottish mountaineering and their names are now given to hills or routes.

MUNROS, CORBETTS AND DONALDS

'Munro-bagging' is becoming an increasingly popular aspect of hillwalking and is now considered by many to be a mountaineering virility symbol, although the converse argument also applies in that the Munro 'bug' can take people away from many attractive hills which do not reach the magic 3,000 ft (914 m). Sir Hugh Munro, Bart, was born not far from Kirriemuir, in Angus, and was one of the original members of the Scottish Mountaineering Club. He was the third president, from 1894 to 1897, and was a regular contributor to the club's journal. In the sixth issue, of September 1891, he presented his 'Tables giving all the Scottish Mountains exceeding 3,000 feet in height'. He did not succeed in climbing all of them himself and died in 1919 aged 63. Sir Hugh listed 283 separate 3,000-ft (914-m) mountains, and in modern times as map-making has improved his list has been altered by SMC committees. Another president of the SMC, the Rev. A. E. Robertson, in 1901 was the first to accomplish the feat of climbing all the Munros of his day, thus setting an enduring habit.

The Munros were followed by a new category, the Corbetts, all Scottish hills over 2,500 ft (700 m) that did not appear in

Opposite: *The village of Torridon*

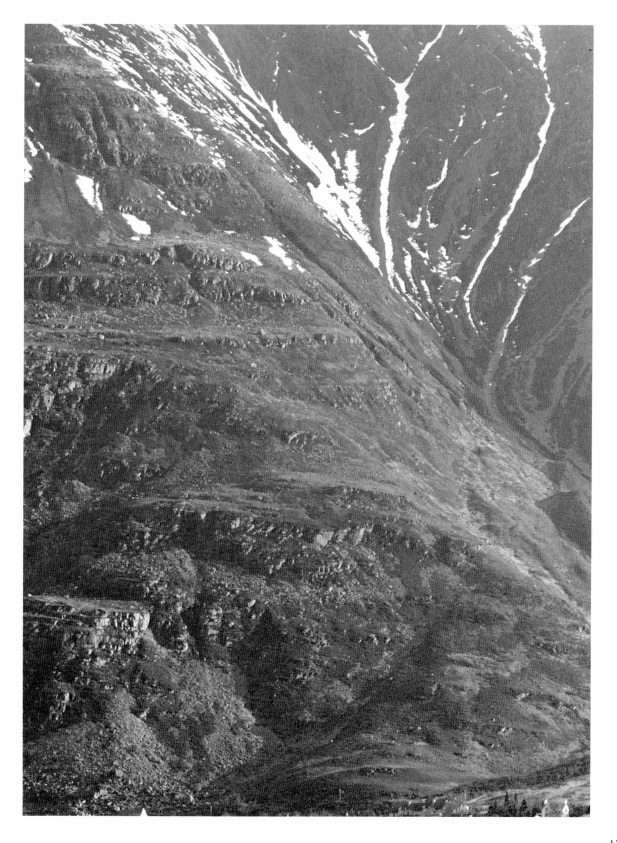

Munro's 'Tables'. They were listed by J. Rooke Corbett, of Bristol, an enthusiastic SMC member and Munroist, and were published after his death in the period following the Second World War. Mr Corbett insisted that his 'Corbetts' should have at least 500 ft (150 m) of ascent on every side and his list of summits has now been upgraded and updated to 221.

There is now a third category, known as the Donalds, all 2,000-ft (610-m) hills in the Lowlands, first formally listed by Percy Donald, also of the SMC.

These categories notwithstanding, one suspects that there is a happy band of people who find categories interesting but a secondary matter, and who enjoy all hills and passes for their own intrinsic appeal.

THE HILL LAND TODAY

What of the face of Scotland's hill land today? In the Highlands much land is still owned by the big estates, which are often in the hands of foreign or absentee owners, and the letting of deer-stalking rights and the sale of venison are essential factors in their economy. Grouse shooting in many areas, including parts of the central belt and the Borders, is also significant. Relations with hill trampers are generally cordial, with most owners respecting people's desire to go to the hills and most walkers and climbers being sensitive to estate needs. This *de facto* pattern of co-existence is a fairly fragile one and no one on either side should be cavalier about it. (See pages 171–2.)

Bulldozed estate roads on the high ground and in the glens have attracted criticism because of landscape being scarred and are often in marked contrast to the skilfully created stalkers' paths of the last century.

Cattle and sheep farming are common in many hill areas and particularly in the Borders, the central belt and parts of the east and north-east. Units tend to be large nowadays and the ruins of smaller farm houses and the croft homes of earlier times can be seen. In the Highlands and Islands crofting is enjoying an upward surge as more young people stay on the land. It is an environmentally healthy pattern and often combined with fishing, tourism, or localized industry. As the old major industries of the central belt, coal, steel, shipbuilding, sadly die out, or are reduced, it is intriguing to note that there are now more members of the Crofters' Union in Scotland than of the National Union of Mineworkers. The distilleries still make use of the hill burns, the old smugglers' tracks often run nearby, and hill and burn water is bottled, canned and exported.

Fish farming has sprung up in many inland and sea lochs, deer farming is being experimented with, and prospecting for minerals, particularly gold, goes on in several hill areas.

Tourism is a major industry in all hill areas and local authorities are now active in producing leaflets about local walks. Most district councils operate Ranger-Naturalist services with financial aid from the Countryside Commission for Scotland and several guiding agencies have been set up.

The period after World War II saw the work of the North of Scotland Hydro Electric Board expand. Its motto is 'Neart nan Gleann', 'power of the glens', and the new reservoirs, dams and lines of pylons greatly changed the scenery in parts of the Highlands. Great efforts were made to be environmentally conscious, not always successfully, and this issue still rages.

But it is the forestry issue which has brought about major scenic change. The depredations of two world wars stimulated planting by the Forestry Commission and new forestry communities sprang up in the Southern Uplands, in the Trossachs, Argyllshire and other areas, providing rural employment and co-existing with the deciduous planting carried out or protected by the private estates, farms and local authorities.

Thirteen per cent of Scotland is now under forestry and the private sector, boosted by modern fiscal benefits and tax concessions for investors, has risen in modern times to account for about half of that. A social and environmental row followed the burgeoning of the private sector and the rate of private forestry investment, and the sale of land for private forestry has now slowed as fiscal benefits were reduced in 1988. Many investors were foreign or not actively interested in forestry as such, acting through agent and representatives. The cash-crop mentality was criticized as being harmful to rural communities through the loss of marginal hill land and there were widespread environmental fears over scenic appearance and harm to wildlife habitat as a result of the blanketing of so many hill and moor areas with monotonous conifer plantations.

Access was also sometimes a problem. Although the Forestry Commission vets private forestry applications, as do the local authorities, little attention was subsequently paid by some developers to known paths or routes and many paths have been buried under trees. The level of rural work provided was debatable and the professed rural social conscience of the developers attacked in the media as merely being just another item in a development portfolio.

The Commission in modern times has paid much attention to scenic planting, mixing the conifer plantations with boundaries or islands of deciduous trees. Also, under the Countryside

(Scotland) Act of 1967, it has promoted recreational facilities and has also tried to honour rights-of-way or traditional passage. The Commission now runs eight camping and caravan sites, 168 picnic places, 292 forest walks or nature trails, seven visitor centres, five arboreta, two forest drives (where cars are allowed) and 87 cabins and holiday homes. A Government-encouraged scheme for scenic tree planting in many parts of the central Lowlands, and particularly on sites left derelict by former industries, announced in the spring of 1989, is one of the most important environmental decisions of recent years and will greatly improve the look of the central belt and enlarge habitats for wild life.

Skiing in Scotland began among hardy individuals in the late nineteenth century and has boomed in modern times, although a series of mild winters has caused problems for developers. The Scottish Ski Club began in 1907 and there are now dozens of clubs. Skiing is taught in many schools and youth groups and the sport continues to boom. Clashes are developing between conservationists and those who want more skiing facilities, but it must also be said that many hillwalkers also ski, and ski-mountaineering or cross-country skiing is now popular.

The Scottish Youth Hostels Association began in 1931 and although many lament the passing of nearly all the small, rough-and-ready hostels in lonely places (some can still be found), the current total of 81 hostels and over 572,220 overnight stays a year shows the popularity of hostelling. The Mountain Bothies Association, a hardy group of volunteers, maintain simple, unlocked cottages in hill areas and in co-operation with the estates who own them.

Formalized training for the outdoors is now a normal part of the scene with the Scottish Centre of Outdoor Training being established at Glen More Lodge in 1948 and now operated by the Scottish Sports Council. Pony trekking has also grown in popularity.

The hardy mountaineer of the Depression years who walked or hitched to hill areas from the cities and slept in caves or home-made howffs (shelters) and the hiking-boom walkers of the 1930s have now been succeeded by hundreds of walkers and climbers who tend to be more affluent as car owning has increased and more clubs organize coaches.

There is occasional concern that the increase in the number of walkers or climbers will cause unbearable pressures, but the size of Scotland relative to its population makes that unlikely other than in some localized spots. Moreover, there are now signs that the total may be levelling out, although no one can be sure.

Conservation bodies doing outstanding work include the Nature Conservancy Council, the Royal Society for the Protection of Birds, the Scottish Wildlife Trust, and the Scottish Ornithological Society. Both the osprey and the sea eagle have returned to Scotland and now breed. The National Trust for Scotland has several mountain properties in its care and there is a Scottish Rights of Way Society and a Scottish Council for Physical Recreation. The Mountaineering Council for Scotland brings together the representatives of many clubs, the Ramblers Association thrives, and Scottish Conservation Projects Trust plant trees, repair paths and bridges and carry out other environmental tasks.

In addition to the Forestry Commission's forest parks, regional or local parks of a semi-wild nature have been set up by regions and districts. There are no national parks in Scotland, an issue which provokes an on-going public debate. The main official, long-distance footpaths set up in modern times by the Countryside Commission and the local authorities, the West Highland Way, and the Southern Upland Way, are the subject of discussion. Supporters say they encourage people to go to the outdoors in safe conditions, ease access, aid tourism and boost the revenue of hotels and hostels. The critics say they promote 'corridor walking', bring restrictions in their wake, are harmful to general access, and tame and erode the ground. The debate continues. The local authorities signpost known paths and there are worries about the disappearance of many of these in urban areas as building work proceeds or farm fields are altered.

Possibly the best time to walk the Scottish hills is in the spring, when the woods and glens are bright green with vibrant new growth, there are blue skies and white snows on the summits, the air is fresh and that scourge of the Highlands, the midge, has not yet emerged in force, the cuckoos are calling in the glens, the oyster-catchers are noisy by the lochsides and rivers and the piping golden plovers and the curlews are calling on the hillside.

INTRODUCTION TO THE ROUTE DESCRIPTIONS

1. ACCESS	See pages 171–2.
2. ASCENT	The amount of climbing involved in each route has been estimated from the Outdoor Leisure or 1:50 000 maps as appropriate and should be regarded as approximate only.
3. CAR-PARKS	The nearest public car-park is given. There will be many places where a car can be parked by the wayside, but it must be done with care, as indiscriminate parking can be a great nuisance to local people.
4. INTERESTING FEATURES ON THE ROUTE	The best position for seeing these is indicated both in the route descriptions and on the maps by *(1)*, *(2)*, etc.
5. LENGTH	These are strictly 'map miles' estimated from the Outdoor Leisure or 1:50 000 maps; no attempt has been made to take into account any ascent or descent involved.
6. MAPS	The maps are drawn to a scale of approximately 1:25 000 or 1:50 000 and all names are as given on Ordnance Survey maps. Field boundaries in particular, which can be a mixture of hedge, fence and wall, should be taken as a 'best description'. The maps have in the main been drawn so that the route goes from the bottom to the top of a page. This will enable the reader to 'line up' the map in the direction walked whilst still holding the book in the normal reading position. The arrow on each map points to grid north. The scale of some small features has been slightly exaggerated for clarity. For easy cross-reference, the relevant Outdoor Leisure and Landranger sheets are indicated on each map.
7. ROUTE DESCRIPTION	The letters 'L' and 'R' stand for left and right respectively. Where these are used for changes of direction then they imply a turn of about 90° when facing in the direction of the walk. 'Half L' and 'half R' indicate a half-turn, i.e. approximately 45°, and 'back half L' or 'back half R' indicate three-quarter turns, i.e. about 135°. PFS stands for 'Public Footpath Sign', PBS for 'Public Bridleway Sign' and OS for 'Ordnance Survey'.

FIGURE 2 *Symbols used on detailed route maps*

To avoid constant repetition, it should be assumed that all stiles and gates mentioned in the route description are to be crossed (unless there is a specific statement to the contrary).

8. STANDARD OF THE ROUTES

The briefest examination of the route descriptions that follow will show that the routes described cover an enormous range of both length and difficulty; the easiest can probably be undertaken by a family party at almost any time of the year whilst the hardest are only really suitable for experienced walkers who are both fit and well-equipped. Any walker therefore who is contemplating following a route should make sure before starting that it is within his or her ability.

It is not easy in practice, however, to give an accurate picture of the difficulty of any route, because it is dependent upon a number of factors and will in any case vary considerably from day to day with the weather. Any consideration of weather conditions must, of course, be left to the walker himself (but read the section on safety first). Apart from that, it is probably best to attempt an overall assessment of difficulty based upon the length, amount of ascent and descent, problems of route-finding and finally, upon the roughness of the terrain.

Each of the routes has therefore been given a grading based upon a consideration of these factors and represented by the bold numerals which precede each walk title. A general description of each grade follows:

Easy (1) Generally short walks (up to 5 miles, 8 km) over well-defined paths, with no problems of route-finding. Some climbing may be involved, but mostly over fairly gradual slopes with only short sections of more difficult ground.

Moderate (2) Rather longer walks (up to about 10 miles, 16 km), mostly over paths, but with sections where route-finding will be more difficult. Mountain summits may be reached with climbing over steeper and rougher ground.

More strenuous (3) Generally longer walks (10–20 miles, 16–32 km), with prolonged spells of climbing. Some rough ground calling for good route-finding ability, perhaps with stretches of scrambling.

Very strenuous (4) Only for the few, involving long distances (over 20 miles, 32 km), with a considerable amount of climbing.

The walks are arranged in order of increasing difficulty within each section.

A summary of each walk is given at the head of each section with information on length, amount of climbing and any special difficulties, such as scrambling, that will be met along the way.

9. STARTING AND FINISHING POINTS

Unless it is stated otherwise, the location of each starting point is given by the number of the appropriate Landranger (1:50 000) map with a six-figure grid reference (see page 174); thus (78-874128) indicates grid reference 874128 which can be found on Landranger sheet no. 78.

10. TIME FOR COMPLETION

The usual method of estimating the length of time needed for a walk is by Naismith's Rule: 'For ordinary walking allow one hour for every 3 miles (5 km) and add one hour for every 2000 feet (600 m) of ascent; for backpacking with a heavy load allow one hour for every 2½ miles (4 km) and one hour for every 1500 feet (450 m) of ascent.' However, for many this tends to be over-optimistic and it is better for each walker to form an assessment of his or her own performance over one or two walks. Naismith's Rule also makes no allowance for rest or food stops or for the influence of weather conditions.

Selected Walks in the Southern Uplands

Richard Mearns

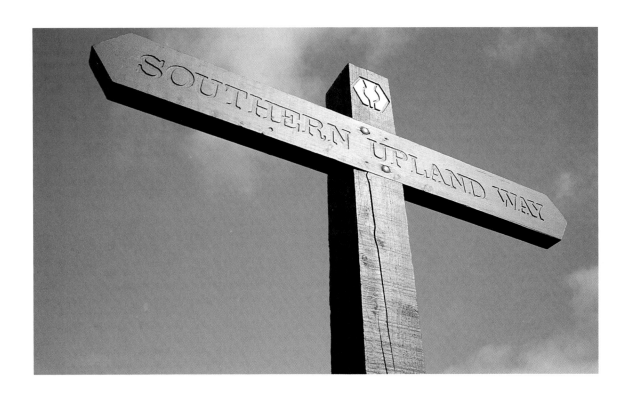

Signpost along the Southern Upland Way

INTRODUCTION

Although chosen for the variety of scenery, length and geographical position, these eight walks reflect my involvement with southern Scotland over the last twenty years. As a student in Edinburgh I often escaped to Holyrood Park and sometimes climbed Arthur's Seat to view the city and the nearby Firth of Forth. Further afield and much less accessible in those days when I lacked a car, St Abb's Head was an exciting prospect, and it remains so for anyone remotely interested in birds. In the summer months the cliffs are thronged with thousands upon thousands of sea-birds.

In 1974, when I moved to Dumfries to begin a nine-year study of peregrines, I had to range all over southern Scotland to the highest and most isolated hills as well as to the long, convoluted coastline—in fact, anywhere there could be nesting cliffs. Each breeding season my travels recommenced, but the first two years were undoubtedly the best because everything then was fresh and exciting. How I wish I had known the landscape before foreign conifers began to dominate the upland areas and change the character of Galloway so severely. However, much that is good remains and I could still have chosen from any number of hill routes. In the end, I have settled on two old favourites, the Merrick and the Grey Mare's Tail. These walks provide splendid introductions to the treeless parts of the Galloway and Moffat hills respectively.

One winter in the 1970s as I waited for spring I studied the roosting and feeding behaviour of the waders on the north Solway shore. It can, of course, be dangerous to wander out across the mudflats but the splendour of the Solway can still be appreciated by climbing Criffel on a clear day to watch the incoming tide surging in over the mud and swirling up the channels and creeks.

When I became the Ranger for the western section of the Southern Upland Way my many years of hill walking meant that I already knew much of the country through which it passes. Two of my walks incorporate tiny portions of this wonderful 212 mile (340 km) coast-to-coast long-distance footpath. The first one includes a tour of the old lead mining village of Wanlockhead and is surely of special interest to all industrial archaeologists and geologists. The other, in Borders Region, makes use of the Minchmoor Road, an ancient trackway which has become a favourite stretch for all Southern Upland Way walkers.

The last walk that I have selected lies just outside my wife's home town of Greenock. The Greenock Cut once supplied water and power to the town; the path beside it now provides an unusual low gradient route suitable for family parties. In the 1820s the walks around the town were described as being among the finest in Europe. Since then Greenock has expanded, not always very attractively, but this is still a fine walk with much of interest and with many outstanding views. Northwards beyond the Clyde the peaks of Ben Lomond and Ben Vorlich give a hint of the type of walking that is available elsewhere in the country.

Rocks near St Abb's Head

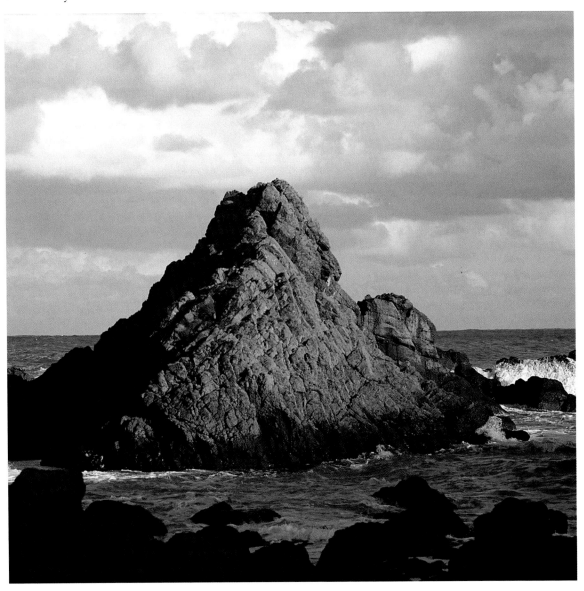

HOLYROOD PARK AND ARTHUR'S SEAT

STARTING AND FINISHING
POINT
Holyrood Palace car-park (66-
270737). Turn R at the lower end of
the Canongate.
LENGTH
2¼ miles (4.5 km)
ASCENT
700 ft (210 m)

This unusual hill-walk offers a wonderful escape from the heart of Edinburgh, less than a mile (1.6 km) away. Holyrood Park's rough moorland areas, precipitous cliffs and shallow lochs provide an agreeable contrast to the surrounding metropolis. There are many paths within the park but this route includes a good many of its historical, geological and wildlife features, as well as the panoramic view from Arthur's Seat.

ROUTE DESCRIPTION (Map 1)

From the car-park beside Holyrood Palace *(1)* cross the road towards the park and turn L up behind the trees beside St Margaret's Well *(2)*. Follow the wide path for about 300 yards (275 m), but as it bends to the R turn half L towards the ruins of St Anthony's Chapel *(3)*. Turn R and follow the bottom of the gorse-lined glen known as the Dry Dam as far as the base of Arthur's Seat *(4)*. The way now turns to the L and climbs to join the well-trod path coming up from Dunsapie Loch. From here it is an easy ascent to the 823 ft (251 m) summit, but take care when you reach it because the rocks have been polished slippery smooth.

From the top, the sudden view of Edinburgh is superb, the Castle and Calton Hill being the most notable features on the skyline. Eastwards, the Lothian coast stretches away towards the Bass Rock in the outer extremities of the Firth of Forth.

To return, begin the descent to Dunsapie Loch but turn R to climb again a little to the top of Crow Hill. From here an indistinct path goes downhill eastwards across several horizontal ridges which are the remains of ancient cultivation terraces. At the road, cross over and follow the pavement around to the R. Below, on the L, is Duddingston Loch and beyond lies Bawsinch Wildlife Reserve *(5)*. The road and pavement contour round the hill but after ½ mile (800 m) they begin to descend to the south end of Salisbury Crags. Leave the pavement and follow the Radical Road *(6)* upwards between the base of the cliffs and the scree slope. It eventually dips down, quite steeply, to bring you back to the car-park.

1 *Holyrood Palace*

Formerly Holyrood Abbey's guest house, the building has developed gradually over the centuries to become the splendid palace which survives today. The greatest number of additions were made by Charles II, who also commissioned the single artist who painted the picture gallery's 111 alleged portraits of Scottish monarchs. Mary Queen of Scots lived here for six years; Bonnie Prince Charlie for just a few months in 1745.

2 *St Margaret's Well*

The structure around the well came from Restalrig, near Portobello. It was moved to its present situation in 1860.

The ruins of St Anthony's Chapel

3 *St Anthony's Chapel*

Only the north wall now survives of a once much larger building. Believed to have been founded in the fifteenth century, it was perhaps built to guard the nearby holy well.

4 *Arthur's Seat*

Arthur's Seat is the remains of a long extinct volcano, some of which has been lost through erosion and some of which is now buried under other, younger rocks. The Castle Rock and Calton Hill are other remnants of the same volcano. Salisbury Crags is an igneous intrusion of very hard basaltic rock.

5 *Duddingston Loch and Bawsinch Wildlife Reserve*

The loch is known for its wintering wildfowl, especially mallard, tufted duck and pochard. A number of other species breed around its edges in summer. Bawsinch was formerly a market garden and scrapyard but was bought in 1971 by the Scottish Wildlife Trust. Since then it has been developed into an unlikely nature reserve acting as a barrier between the city and Duddingston Loch Bird Sanctuary.

6 *Radical Road*

The road takes its name from a group of destitute radical weavers from the west of Scotland who were collected together in 1820 by Sir Walter Scott and a few friends to improve the boulder-strewn trackway.

Looking towards the centre of Edinburgh from St Anthony's Chapel

1.2

St Abb's Head

STARTING AND FINISHING
POINT
Northfield Farm Visitor Centre (67-
913674). On the B6438 between
Coldingham and St Abbs.
LENGTH
3½ miles (5.5 km)
ASCENT
400 ft (120 m).

These awesome cliffs rise up nearly 300 ft (90 m) above the North Sea, and hold one of the largest concentrations of breeding sea-birds on the east coast of mainland Britain. The best time to see the birds is in spring and early summer, but this easy walk is dramatic at all times of year.

Route Description (Map 2)

The first part of the walk is clearly waymarked. From the Visitor Centre *(1)* continue downhill to a stile beside the B6438. Turn half L across the farm entrance to a gap in the wall where four steps lead down to the start of a fenced path which runs parallel with the road. Turn L after 250 yards (225 m) when the path meets a high wall with an information board. After passing through two kissing-gates the first good views of the red sandstone seacliffs begin to unfold and the air can be filled with the sight, sound and smell of sea-birds *(2)*. Continue along the cliff-top path, remembering to look back from time to time towards the village and harbour of St Abbs *(3)*, and the cliffs leading southwards to Eyemouth.

At Horsecastle Bay there is a stile. Turn L along the upper side of the fence to the outside corner of the field where the closely cropped grassy path becomes indistinct. Turn half R up the gully bottom which leads to the cliff edge again, keeping an eye out in summer for the flowers of the common rock rose.

Join the metalled road at the lighthouse *(4)* and follow it down towards Pettico Wick. On rounding the first sharp bend, you will have a sudden view of flat-topped cliffs stretching away northwards to Fast Castle and beyond. In the distance the Bass Rock rises precipitously from the Firth of Forth, and on clear days the low flat Isle of May can be seen further eastwards, with the Kingdom of Fife beyond.

At the lowest point in the road, turn L and follow the narrow path down the L (eastern) side of the Mire Loch *(5)*. Carry on beyond the dam to the fence and turn L along it to rejoin the path which leads back to the car-park.

Pettico Wick

1 Visitor Centre

St Abb's Head National Nature Reserve was purchased in 1980 by the National Trust for Scotland, which administers it as a wildlife reserve in conjunction with the Scottish Wildlife Trust. Jointly, they provide a Ranger service. The newly created Visitor Centre offers information on the fauna and flora of the area, including taped sea-bird noises.

2 Sea-birds

The towering cliffs offer nesting ledges to a host of sea-birds, the most numerous being guillemots and kittiwakes, each of which species numbers in excess of 10,000 pairs. There are

PATHFINDER NT 86/96   **MAP 2**

ST ABB'S HEAD LIGHTHOUSE ④

PETTICO WICK

⑤ MIRE LOCH

KIRK HILL

HORSECASTLE BAY

N

STILE

②

KISSING GATES

NORTHFIELD FARM

STILE

STARTING AND FINISHING POINT

① ST ABBS ③

HARBOUR

SCALE 1:25000

also razorbills, shags, fulmars, herring gulls and a few puffins. Gannets do not breed here but thousands pass offshore, to and from the Bass Rock.

3 St Abbs

The village is named after St Aebba who founded a church here in the seventh century. The present church and harbour were built by a member of the brewing family of Usher who stipulated, despite his business, that there should be no public house here—and the village still lacks one.

4 St Abb's Head Lighthouse

The light was built in 1862 to help safeguard shipping on this storm-battered coast. But so great was the gale of 14 October 1881 that half the fishing fleet of Eyemouth (24 boats) sank, with the loss of 129 lives.

5 The Mire Loch

This artificial loch was constructed in 1901 for trout fishing. Gulls, coots, mallards, goldeneyes and tufted ducks may be seen here in the autumn and winter, if the water does not freeze.

1.3

THE GREENOCK CUT

STARTING AND FINISHING
POINT
Cornalees Bridge Visitor Centre (63-
246722). Turn east off the A742
Greenock-Inverkip road to Loch
Thom.
LENGTH
7½ miles (12 km)
ASCENT
300 ft (90 m)

This easy circular walk follows an old aqueduct from the Cornalees Bridge Visitor Centre to the outskirts of Greenock and returns over the moors past Loch Thom. There are interesting views northwards across the Firth of Clyde and south-westwards to Arran and Bute.

ROUTE DESCRIPTION (Map 3)

From the car-park at the Visitor Centre (1) follow the signs to the nature trail by turning R and then immediately L across the old Cornalees Bridge. Go through a metal gate on the R and down the concrete steps to the sluice-gates. The far one, with the wooden walkway, used to help control the water levels in the Greenock Cut (2). Pass to the L of it and follow the narrow aqueduct for the next 5½ miles (9 km), always keeping it on your R. There are a number of metal kissing-gates along the route, but the way is always obvious. The first gate is reached after ¼ mile (400 m), and 20 yards (18 m) beyond it the nature trail forks off to the L across a stile. By following the Cut you will soon come to Shielhill Farm (3), where there are two gates on opposite sides of the metalled road. Once clear of the first field and a short wooded section, you will have views on the L of Arran, Bute and the outer Clyde.

Along the Cut there are several navvies' stone huts (4) which date from the time that the channel was cut. The path seems to follow the same contour but in fact drops gradually downhill all the way to Overton Long Dam, where a road crosses the Cut beside a cottage. Turn R across the bridge and go through yet another metal kissing-gate. The rough track skirts the edges of two small reservoirs before climbing gently uphill. Looking back, there are views of the urban sprawl of Greenock, its redundant shipyard cranes, the Clyde and distant Ben Lomond. The large, prominent, dark-brick building is the Inverclyde Royal Hospital. One feature not shown on your map is an elliptical 'sandbank' lying between Greenock and Helensburgh.

Previous page: *The harbour at St Abb's*

MAP 3

GREENOCK

OVERTON DAM

PATHFINDER
NS 27/37

SCALE 1:25000

KISSING GATE

HUT

GATE

N

HUT

LOCH THOM

5

LOCH THOM COTTAGE

DAM

COMPENSATION RESERVOIR

HUT

STARTING AND FINISHING POINT

CORNALEES VISITOR CENTRE CAR PARK

1

LAVEROCKHOUSE △ HILL 293m

KISSING GATES

4

SHIELHILL FARM

3

HUT

HUT

GREENOCK CUT

2

Greenock Cut sluice mechanism

37

This is the upturned, rusting hull of a Greek sugar ship which capsized in 1974.

A mile (1.6 km) from Overton, Loch Thom (5) and the smaller Compensation Reservoir come into view. From Loch Thom Cottage the road leads directly back to the car-park.

1 *Cornalees Bridge Visitor Centre*
Opened in July 1973, this Visitor Centre is the third stage in growth of the 35,000-acre (14,165 hectares) Clyde-Muirshiel Regional Park. There is a Ranger Service and a signposted circular nature trail down the wooded Shielhill Glen. The lower section of the glen is now a Site of Special Scientific Interest, yet until 160 years ago it was an active quarry which supplied the sandstone for many of Greenock's buildings.

2 *Greenock Cut*
Foreign shipping, the lack of a sewerage system and a severely inadequate water supply combined to make Greenock the unhealthiest town in Scotland in the nineteenth century. The town was expanding rapidly and the demand for fresh water increased, so the Greenock Cut was devised to alleviate some of the town's problems. From 1827, the aqueduct supplied fresh water and also provided water power to as many as twenty-six factories on the eastern fall-line from Overton Long Dam. In sharp contrast to the Cut, which only drops 27 ft (8 m) in 5½ miles (9 km), the fall-line drops 512 ft (156 m) between Overton and the Clyde.

3 *Shielhill Farm*
The Ranger Service occasionally takes parties down to the farm so that they can watch, from a special viewing platform, the cows being milked.

4 *Navvies' huts*
The Shaws Water Joint Stock Company guaranteed a flow of 1200 cubic ft (33,980 l) of water per minute for twelve hours a day down the eastern fall-line. Navvies used the stone shelters, especially during the difficult task of winter maintenance as they struggled to keep the channel free of snow and ice.

5 *Loch Thom*
Originally known as the Little Caspian, the loch was renamed to commemorate Robert Thom who had the vision to bring the water around Dunrod Hill to Greenock. In 1971 a 1¼-mile (2 km) tunnel linked the reservoir with the town and Thom's Greenock Cut became obsolete after 144 years of use. It is now a scheduled Ancient Monument.

Looking towards Loch Thom Cottage

Grey Mare's Tail and Loch Skeen

STARTING AND FINISHING POINT

National Trust for Scotland car-park (79-186145). 5 miles (8 km) south-west of St Mary's Loch on the A708 Moffat–Selkirk road.

LENGTH

6 miles (9.5 km)

ASCENT

1900 ft (580 m).

Impressive views of the Grey Mare's Tail waterfall, an isolated hill loch and the surrounding craggy hills, combine to make this walk the scenic rival of many a route in the western Highlands. Owned by the National Trust for Scotland, it provides an excellent introduction to the Moffat hills where open moorland is still predominantly managed for sheep.

ROUTE DESCRIPTION (Map 4)

From the information shelter beside the walled car-park, two paths are clearly visible. One leads only to the base of the Grey Mare's Tail (1). The other, which cuts diagonally across the hillside to the north, is the route to be taken for Loch Skeen. Cross the Tail Burn by the road bridge, turn half L and head up the steps to an old sheep enclosure where information boards explain the local geology and Charles Lapworth's interest in it (2). The path from here to the loch is obvious and easy to follow, but do not stray from it in an attempt to get a better look at the falls: the grassy slopes are slippery and have claimed a number of lives.

The majority of visitors to Loch Skeen (3) stop at the water's edge and if it is misty on the higher ground it is advisable that you also turn back here. But on good days the high circuit around the loch is well worthwhile and can be very dramatic.

To climb higher, turn L over the makeshift ford beside the loch, skirt around the lower end of the loch and head north-west towards the prominent conical hill ahead. Follow the faint zig-zag path up it, keeping well away from the precipices of Mid Craig on the R. At the summit follow magnetic bearing 295° for 750 yards (700 m) to meet a fence, with a ruined wall behind. Turn R and follow the fence to Firthybrigg Head, then down to Talla Nick and up again to the plateau of Lochcraig Head (2625 ft, 800 m). From here there are excellent views down to Loch

Waterfall on the Tail Burn

Skeen. To the west, north and east are the Lowther, Moorfoot and Eildon Hills respectively.

To return, continue to follow the same fence as it leads steeply downhill. On the more level ground east of the loch carefully negotiate the driest possible route through the peat hags, a good area for cloudberries in some autumns. When the fence turns sharp L, turn R down to the loch shore and follow the water's edge southwards until the path leading up from the car-park is rejoined.

1 Grey Mare's Tail

During the last Ice Age, when this area was covered in glaciers, the larger, faster glacier in the Moffat Water gouged out a deeper valley than the glacier in the Tail Burn where Loch Skeen now lies. This created a classic 'hanging valley': the Tail Burn must now plunge 200 feet (60 m) to join the Moffat Water.

2 Charles Lapworth

Charles Lapworth (1842–1920) is well known to geologists. He lived for a while at Birkhill, the first cottage on the R on the road from the car-park to St Mary's Loch. He made a special study of fossil graptolites here and at Raking Gill beside Birkhill.

3 Loch Skeen

The alternative spelling 'Loch Skene' is still sometimes used. At the beginning of the last century white-tailed sea eagles were said to breed here.

In 1962, 2383 acres (964 hectares) of land surrounding the loch were purchased by the National Trust for Scotland, and ten years later a further 128 acres (52 hectares) were added. There is a Ranger service in July and August.

Loch Skeen

WANLOCKHEAD AND LOWTHER HILL

STARTING AND FINISHING
POINT
Museum of Scottish Lead Mining car-park, Wanlockhead (78-874128).
Turn south off the A74 at Abingdon or Elvanfoot; or turn north off the A76 at Mennock.
LENGTH
6½ miles (10.5 km)
ASCENT
1230 ft (375 m)

At 1394 ft (425 m), Wanlockhead is the highest inhabited village in Scotland. It is not very pretty but it has a unique character and is intriguing because of the long tradition of lead mining here since perhaps Roman times. Even though there is now little mining, there are still many associated places of interest in and around the village. The spur along part of the Southern Upland Way to the summit of Lowther Hill (2378 ft, 725 m) is an easy waymarked walk to a high viewpoint.

ROUTE DESCRIPTION (Map 5)

Cross the road beside the car-park at the museum (1) and follow the Southern Upland Way (2) downhill along the former track of a narrow-gauge railway. On the R, just across the Wanlock Water, is the Loch Nell Mine (3) and 250 yards (225 m) downstream there is a large old beam engine (4). After ⅝ mile (1 km) turn R up onto the metalled road. Turn L but leave the road (and the Southern Upland Way) by turning R 50 yards (45 m) before Meadowfoot Cemetery (5).

Follow the narrow gravel path up to the old mine workings, where Symington's engine once stood (6). Turn back half R down the track to the road and turn L towards the centre of Wanlockhead. After ¼ mile (400 m) the road passes the Straitsteps miners' cottages and the beam engine. Three hundred yards (275 m) beyond the church, take the L fork in the road which leads uphill past the library (7) and youth hostel. Continue on up to the B979 and cross straight over to the old railway line (8) which lies parallel to the road. Follow the embankment along to the R to the Walk Inn where the Southern Upland Way is rejoined.

If you visited the museum, mine, miners' cottages and miners' library you will have learnt much about the history of the village. It is now time to concentrate on the route up Lowther Hill and to see the surrounding countryside.

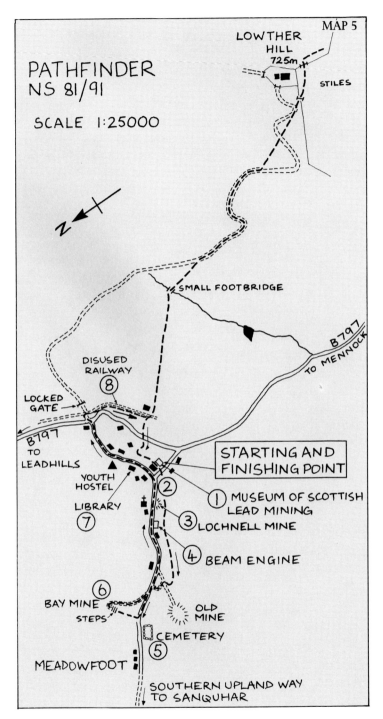

PATHFINDER
NS 81/91

SCALE 1:25000

MAP 5

LOWTHER HILL
725m

STILES

SMALL FOOTBRIDGE

B797 TO MENNOCK

DISUSED RAILWAY
⑧

LOCKED GATE

B797 TO LEADHILLS

YOUTH HOSTEL

LIBRARY
⑦

STARTING AND FINISHING POINT

②

① MUSEUM OF SCOTTISH LEAD MINING

③ LOCHNELL MINE

④ BEAM ENGINE

⑥ BAY MINE

STEPS

OLD MINE

CEMETERY
⑤

MEADOWFOOT

SOUTHERN UPLAND WAY TO SANQUHAR

Lowther Hill

Turn L at the Walk Inn, following the fingerposts and waymarks. After a 1-mile (1.6-km) moorland section, the Way joins the metalled service road for the Civil Aviation Authority's radar station, but leaves it from time to time to take the shorter but steeper route to the summit.

On clear days there are splendid views down Nithsdale to Criffel, as well as to the Isle of Man and even to the Paps of Jura, 95 miles (153 km) to the north-west. To obtain additional views to the east, cross the ladder stile beside the radar station and continue along the path for 200 yards (180 m) to a second stile.

On the descent, by the same route, the patchwork effect of the hillsides around Wanlockhead is very noticeable. It has been created by controlled burning of the heather to provide the best variety of food and shelter for red grouse. From the Walk Inn follow the Southern Upland Way signs down to the car-park.

Meadowfoot Cemetery (Wanlockhead)

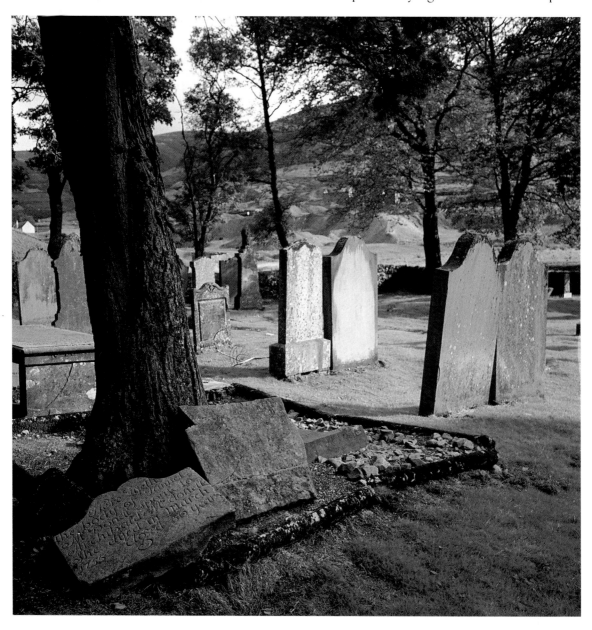

1 Museum of Scottish Lead Mining

Displays and an audio-visual programme reveal some of the history of this unusual Scottish village and show some of the difficulties faced by the miners. The mineral collection indicates that not only lead but also gold, silver, zinc and antimony have been extracted locally.

2 Southern Upland Way

This 212-mile (340-km) coast-to-coast long-distance foot-path traverses some of Dumfries and Galloway's finest scenery. Starting in the west at Portpatrick, it passes through Castle Kennedy, Glentrool, St John's Town of Dalry, Sanquhar, Wanlockhead and Beattock before heading into the Borders to finish at Cockburnspath, overlooking the North Sea.

3 Loch Nell Mine

First opened in 1710, the mine's present-day visitors are issued with helmets and guided in for about 300 yards (275 m) to view veins of ore, a deep vertical shaft and a tableau of wax models at the rock face. Open Easter–September.

4 Wanlockhead Beam Engine

The only water-powered beam engine of its kind to survive in such good condition, it was used to drain the Straitsteps Mine and was capable of raising water from 88 ft (27 m) below ground. The museum contains a working model.

5 Meadowfoot Cemetery

Besides demonstrating that trees will grow quite well in this region if left alone by man and sheep, the walled enclosure contains an interesting assortment of memorials to the professions of the past. Miners, smelters, blacksmiths and teachers all lie buried here.

6 Symington's Engine

William Symington's first commercial atmospheric pumping engine stood here from 1790 to 1799 in an attempt to combat the recurrent flooding problem of the Bay Mine. Symington was born in the neighbouring village of Leadhills and later pioneered steam navigation.

7 Wanlockhead Miners' Library

Dating from 1756, the library is the second oldest subscription library in Britain, preceded only by the one in nearby Leadhills. A plaque on the wall commemorates the poet Robert Reid, who was born here in 1850.

8 Wanlockhead Railway

A spur from Elvanfoot, on the main Glasgow–Carlisle line, reached Leadhills in 1901 and Wanlockhead in 1902, carrying passengers as well as minerals. It was closed just before World War II.

2.6

NEW ABBEY and CRIFFEL

STARTING AND FINISHING
POINT
The Abbey car-park, New Abbey (84-964663), 6 miles (9.5 km) south of
Dumfries on the A710.
LENGTH
6¾ miles (11 km)
ASCENT
1800 ft (550 m)

From the warm-red sandstone ruins of New Abbey, the early part of this walk passes through farmland, mixed and coniferous woodland, and ascends to the heather-clad slopes of Criffel. The summit overlooks the Solway Firth, the last unspoilt major estuary in Europe and the only one with such a fine viewpoint.

ROUTE DESCRIPTION (Map 6)

From the car-park beside Sweetheart Abbey *(1)* go back to the main road and turn R towards the village centre. Turn half L at the Abbey Arms along the road behind the Corn Mill *(2)*. After 40 yards (35 m) turn L so that the mill pond is on your R. The road soon bends to the R and shortly after, on the L, are five granite steps between two yew trees. Go through the kissing-gate to a field, keeping to the L along the hedge to a second such gate. Follow the road ahead for ¾ mile (1.2 km) to a crossroads.

A signpost points the way up to the Waterloo Monument *(3)* but those heading for Criffel should turn L across the sleeper bridge. Pass behind the Mid Glen Cottage, following the rough track beside the tree-lined Glen Burn to a gate and stile. Turn L keeping to the track until it joins a well-defined forest road. Turn R, but leave this road to the L at the second sharp bend, passing along the top of the conifer plantation to a wall. Follow it up the hill for ¾ mile (1.2 km), taking note of a tumbled-down wall that you cross. When the good wall bears L, a fence bears to the R. Bisect the angle between them and follow the ill-defined path through the heather to the summit of Knocken-doch. From here there are good views back to the Abbey and a little to the west of it, among the trees, is Shambellie House *(4)*. Below Knockendoch lies kidney-shaped Loch Kindar *(5)* beyond which is the Nith Estuary.

If visibility is poor there is little point in continuing along the ridge to the summit of Criffel (1867 ft/569 m), but in good conditions the extra mile (1.6 km) will reward the walker with views of Carsethorn *(6)*, the whole of the inner Solway *(7)*, and further afield, the Lake District and Isle of Man.

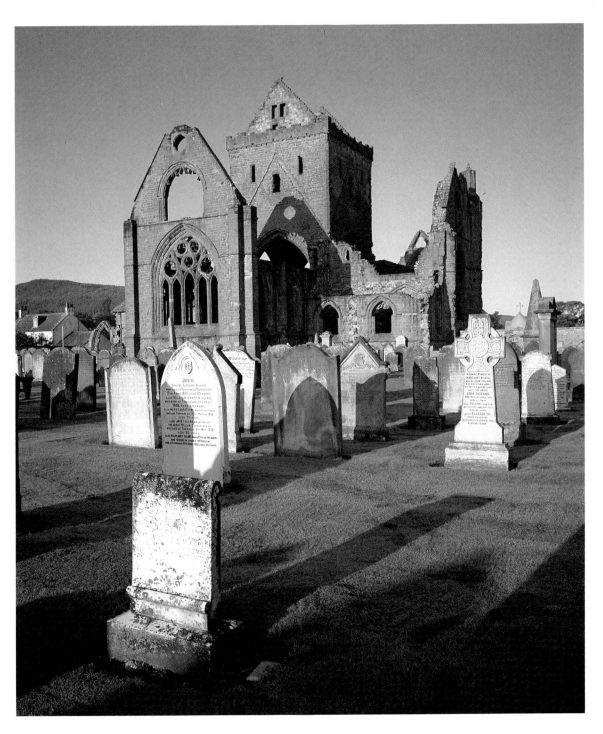

Sweetheart Abbey

Return to Knockendoch and descend as far as the previously mentioned fallen wall. Turn L, following the stones down to the forest road (turn half L for the last 10 yards/9 m to avoid the deep ditch). Turn R and follow the roadway for 1½ miles (2.5 km) to the edge of New Abbey. At the edge of the housing

View from Criffel

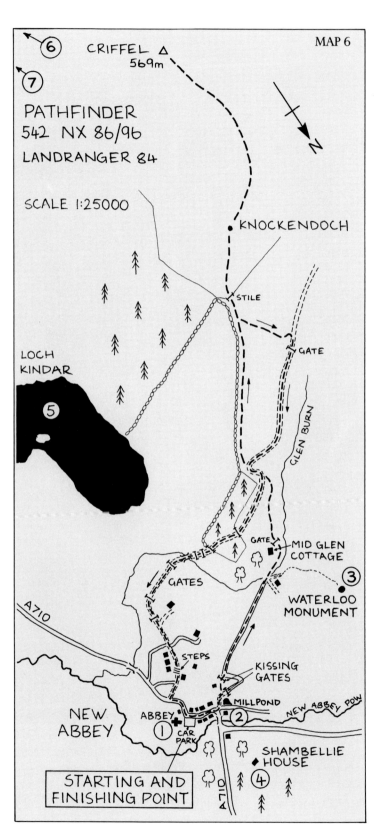

estate, turn back half L immediately after passing between two white gate pillars. After 10 yards (9 m) there is a granite stile on the R. Follow the narrow, wooded path behind the houses, descend the twelve stone steps behind an old mill and head between high hedges across the drive to the concrete path which crosses a field to the main road. Cross over the road, turn L, and take the pavement back to the Abbey.

1 *Sweetheart Abbey*

Founded in 1273, the Abbey was 'new' in relation to that of Dundrennan, the mother house founded 130 years earlier 18 miles (29 km) to the south-west. It is known as Sweetheart Abbey because its founder, the widowed Devorgilla Balliol, kept her husband's heart for 16 years in an ivory and silver casket and was buried here with it.

2 *Corn Mill*

There has been a mill on this site since the busy days of the Abbey. The present nineteenth-century mill was in use until 1947 and has recently been restored. The wheel on the west wall is of the high breastshot or pitchback type.

3 *Waterloo Monument*

Construction began on 6 October 1815, less than four months after Napoleon's final defeat. The money was raised by public subscription and the ground was given by William Stewart of Shambellie, whose brother James had commanded the Black Watch 42nd Foot at Waterloo.

4 *Shambellie House*

This Victorian mansion in Scottish baronial style is now a Museum of Costume run by the National Museum of Scotland. Admission is free.

5 *Loch Kindar*

The larger wooded isle is the site of Kirk Kindar; the smaller is the site of an ancient crannog. Large numbers of mute swans come here in the autumn to moult.

6 *Carsethorn*

This quiet fishing village still boasts a ruinous wooden jetty which recalls its busier days. In 1850 10,000 emigrants left here for Canada and 11,000 for Australia and New Zealand.

7 *Solway Firth*

The mudflats and adjacent saltmarshes of the inner Solway are of international importance as the feeding grounds for several species of geese, ducks and waders. The entire population of barnacle geese from Spitzbergen, in the Norwegian islands of Svalbard, winters here, mainly at Caerlaverock and Rockcliffe Marshes. More than 20,000 oystercatchers spend mid-winter on these shores.

3.7

THE MERRICK

STARTING AND FINISHING
POINT
Bruce's Stone car-park, Glentrool
(77-415804). At Bargrennan turn
north off the A714 to Glentrool
village. Turn east for 3¾ miles (6 km)
to the end of the metalled road.
LENGTH
10 miles (16 km)
ASCENT
2300 ft (700 m).

After climbing to the highest point in southern Scotland, the
return route skirts the shores of three rugged hill lochs then
descends the slopes of Glentrool to finish with a delightful oak-
lined section with a waterfall. The walk provides a good
introduction to the Galloway hills but here and elsewhere in the
Southern Uplands the difficulties should not be underestimated.

ROUTE DESCRIPTION (Maps 7, 8)

Follow the path northwards from Bruce's Stone (1) along the
west side of the Buchan Burn. The early part of the way is
signposted so there should be no difficulty. At the second stile
the route passes through a conifer plantation for ½ mile (800 m)
until the ruin of Culsharg is reached. Go to the left of the
building, heading uphill to a forest road. Turn R across the
concrete bridge but 25 yards (20 m) later turn L up a gravelly
slope into the trees once more.

After the stile above the trees continue upwards to a wall,
turning R to follow it to the top of Benyellary. On good days the
Mull of Galloway, Ailsa Craig and Arran can be seen.

From Benyellary continue beside the wall for ⅝ mile (1 km)
then turn half R along the faint path which leads to the Merrick
summit (2770 ft/843 m).

East of the Merrick there is a wonderful assortment of
waters. Loch Doon to the north and Clatteringshaws to the
south-east were both artificially dammed in the 1930s as part of
the Galloway hydro-electric scheme. Closer to hand, Loch
Enoch (2) and her sister lochs give this area its special beauty.

There is no path for the descent to the fence at the south-
west corner of Loch Enoch, but the vegetation is short and
easily managed if care is taken. At the stile by the shore a 400-
yard (375 m) diversion up the fence will give, after a little
searching, a sighting of the Grey Man of the Merrick.

Returning to the loch, turn R and walk along the shore until
it heads northwards abruptly. Turn R here and follow the

PATHFINDER
515 NX 48/58

SCALE 1:25000

MAP 7
CONTINUE ON MAP 8

BENYELLARY CAIRN 719m

N

STILE

WHITELAND BURN

BUCHAN BURN

CULSHARG

STILE

CONTINUED FROM MAP 8

STILE

STARTING AND FINISHING POINT

WATERFALLS

GATES

MARTYR'S TOMB
④

CAR PARK

⑤

BRUCE'S STONE
①

BUCHAN HOUSE

GAIRLAND BURN

LOCH TROOL

narrow pass towards Loch Neldricken. The path now becomes obvious again. Skirt to the west of the Murder Hole *(3)* and follow the path towards Loch Valley, afterwards keeping to the west bank of the Gairland Burn. The route is wet in places, but

Buchan Burn

the path improves as it begins to contour around the side of
Buchan Hill to a wall. Just off the path, the rocky knoll beyond
the gate is a good view-point for Loch Trool. In the woods at
the far end is the Martyrs' Tomb at Caldons *(4)*.

The path back remains on the north side of the wall for 250 yards (225 m) then enters the field by a small gate. Turn half R and go downhill to the field corner, where there is another small gate. At the stile beside the next gate turn R along the track which leads through the oak woods back to Bruce's Stone. It is worth pausing at the Buchan Bridge (5) and for those with the energy a 200-yard (180-m) excursion up the path on the east bank leads to one of Galloway's most spectacular waterfalls.

Deserted Culsharg

1 *Bruce's Stone*

The large granite boulder is inscribed: 'In loyal remembrance of Robert the Bruce, King of Scots, whose victory in this glen over an English force in March, 1307, opened the campaign of independence which he brought to a decisive close at Bannockburn on 24th June, 1314.'

The stone was erected in 1929, 600 years after Bruce's death. The battle took place on the other side of the loch, where a small band of Scots hurled boulders down the hillside and routed Sir Aymer de Valence's 2,000 men.

2 *Loch Enoch*

The silver sand from the loch's beaches was once prized as a coating for greased wooden hone sticks, used for sharpening scythes.

A feature of this loch is an island with its own lochan.

3 *The Murder Hole*

This marshy dark-water bay of Loch Neldricken features in S. R. Crockett's novel *The Raiders* as a site for concealing stolen goods and the bodies of the thieves' victims. The Galloway-born author's other works include *Men of the Moss Hags* and *Mad Sir Uchtred*.

4 *The Martyrs' Tomb*

South-west Scotland was the scene of many bloody acts during the 'Killing Times'. Seventeenth-century Scottish Presbyterians objected to having the English Episcopalian form of worship thrust upon them, so their leaders signed the rebellious National Covenant in 1638. Many took to the hills to hold their services. The Martyrs' Tomb commemorates six such Covenanters surprised at prayer and shot by dragoons.

5 *Buchan Bridge*

This small sandstone bridge was designed by Randolph, 9th Earl of Galloway. Part of the inscription alludes, in the words of Sir Walter Scott, to the surrounding 'Land of the Brown Heath and Shaggy Wood, Land of the Mountain and the Flood.'

THE MINCHMOOR ROAD

STARTING AND FINISHING
POINT
Traquair village-hall car-park (73-
332346). Turn L off the B709 from
Innerleithen at the Traquair war
memorial. The village hall is 100 yards
(90 m) along on the L.
LENGTH
16 miles (26 km)
ASCENT
2300 ft (700 m)

Much of the Border country is rich in history and this area is no exception. The route is mainly a ridge walk along an old drove road (and the Southern Upland Way) from Traquair to the Three Brethren. The return via Broadmeadows makes use of the Minchmoor Road. The path surface is generally excellent.

ROUTE DESCRIPTION (Maps 9–11)

From Traquair village hall turn L away from the main road uphill for 150 yards (140 m) until the road bends to the R. Continue straight ahead, following the rough trackway signposted 'Minchmoor'. Carry on up between the widely spaced walls of the old drove road which led to Galashiels and Selkirk. The route should now be clear for 7 miles (11 km) all the way to the Three Brethren, since Southern Upland Way *(1)* signs clarify any doubtful sections.

At 1500 ft (460 m) the track starts to contour round the heathery north side of Minch Moor, 1859 ft (567 m), passing just to the left of the ancient Cheese Well *(2)*. Continue along the ridge for 1½ miles (2.5 km) to Hare Law where the drove road and Minchmoor Road divide. Fork L, continuing to follow the Southern Upland Way signs. After ½ mile (800 m) the track passes through an ancient ditch and embankment known as Wallace's Trench *(3)*.

Beyond Brown Knowe the path becomes narrow and descends to a ladder stile at the west end of a windblown shelter belt of larch and pine. Keeping the trees on your R, carry on eastwards along the grassy track which skirts to the north of Broomy Law, enjoying all the while the open views of the rolling Border hills.

At the new plantation which appears on the L, follow the rough track until it joins a well-used forest road which leads up to the Three Brethren: three tall, closely placed cairns, each on ground of different ownership. As you look eastwards, the best views of the three Eildon Hills are now obtained.

A Southern Upland Way fingerpost indicates the route

MAP 9

CONTINUE ON MAP 10

HARELAW •

PATHFINDER 460
NT 23/33

SCALE 1:25000

Z

MINCHMOOR
△ 567m

CHEESE
WELL
②

STILE AND GATE

GATES

STARTING AND
FINISHING POINT
①

B709

NEW HOUSE

TRAQUAIR
HOUSE
⑧

WAR MEMORIAL

TRAQUAIR

Right: *Beech trees at Yarrowford.* Far Right: *The Three Brethren* downhill to the R, but as the Way bears L into the trees, turn R through the gate. Join the track beside the gate, turn R along it for 10 yards (9 m), then turn R again to double back almost parallel to the fence, but veer slightly L from it. The path ahead is very overgrown with heather but after 500 yards (450 m) there is a gate beyond which the track is clearly visible, and it remains so. From the col ahead there is a steep descent from the high moors down to the Yarrow valley, to a small wood where a L turn leads directly towards the ruins of Newark Castle *(4)*.

From the gate beside the A708 it is only ¼ mile (400 m) eastwards to Foulshiels, the ruined birthplace of the explorer Mungo Park *(5)*, but those walkers keeping to the route should turn R into Broadmeadows *(6)*, crossing two bridges over the Yarrow Water twice within ¼ mile (400 m).

From the second bridge it is 600 yards (550 m) until the Minchmoor is signposted to the R. The narrow road soon becomes a rough track which leads up behind some red-roofed garages. Turn L at the first junction, beside some magnificent old beech trees. Once above the trees turn L along the north side of the wood and enjoy the gentle uphill gradient of the old Minchmoor Road *(7)*, with its splendid wide grassy surface, open outlook and historic associations with the past.

At Hare Law rejoin the Southern Upland Way and follow it back to Traquair. By now walkers will be travelling at a more leisurely pace than that of the Marquis of Montrose when he fled along the Minchmoor Road on his way to Traquair House *(8)*. The house may be glimpsed among the trees on the descent to the finishing point.

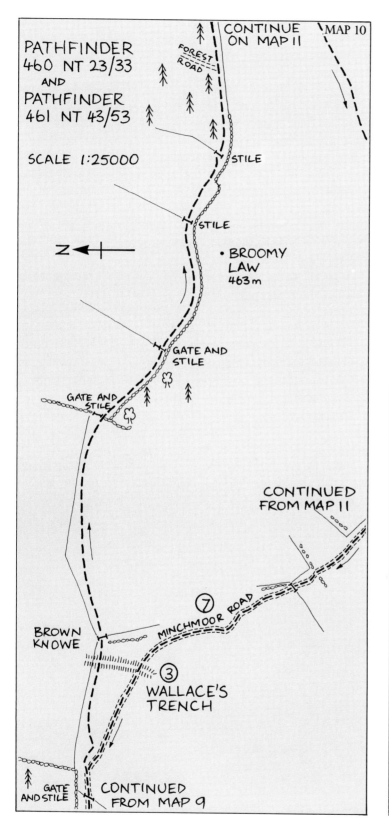

PATHFINDER
460 NT 23/33
AND
PATHFINDER
461 NT 43/53

SCALE 1:25000

MAP 10

CONTINUE
ON MAP 11

FOREST
ROAD

STILE

STILE

• BROOMY
LAW
463 m

Z

GATE AND
STILE

GATE AND
STILE

CONTINUED
FROM MAP 11

⑦

MINCHMOOR ROAD

BROWN
KNOWE

③
WALLACE'S
TRENCH

GATE
AND STILE

CONTINUED
FROM MAP 9

CONTINUED FROM MAP 10

CONTINUE ON MAP 9

Beech trees at Yarrowford

61

1 Southern Upland Way

See note 2 on page 47.

2 Cheese Well

The spring is marked by two stones, one dated 1965, the other much older. By tradition travellers made an offering of cheese to placate the fairies or spirits of the well, to ensure protection on the Minchmoor Road.

3 Wallace's Trench

This linear earthwork lies across both the Minchmoor Road and the old drove road. It may have had an administrative rather than defensive purpose and probably had no connection with the popular hero William Wallace.

4 Newark Castle

The courtyard of this fifteenth-century square tower was the scene of a dreadful slaughter of Royalist prisoners after the Battle of Philiphaugh in 1645. Much later, it was visited by Sir Walter Scott and William Wordsworth together, and featured in Scott's *Lay of the Last Minstrel*.

5 Mungo Park

Born in 1771, Park studied medicine in Edinburgh and between his two African expeditions practised in Peebles 13 miles (21 km) north-west of Foulshiels. There were no white survivors of his second great journey (in 1806) but Park is believed to have drowned in the Niger while being attacked by natives.

6 Broadmeadows

The Scottish Youth Hostel Association is responsible for over 80 hostels. The first to be opened, in 1931, was at Broadmeadows, the opening party crossing the Minchmoor to complete the ceremony.

7 The Minchmoor Road

This trackway has been in use since at least the thirteenth century as it was part of the road between Kelso Abbey and its lands at Lesmahagow. In 1296 Edward I and his army used the road during his campaign against the Scots.

Four centuries later, the Marquis of Montrose galloped along this road to bang on the door of Traquair House, after his defeat at Philiphaugh by General Leslie's Covenanting army. He was refused admission but eventually escaped to Norway.

8 Traquair House

Visited by twenty-seven kings, Traquair House claims to be the oldest inhabited house in Scotland. The main block dates from 1642, about the time that the 1st Earl of Traquair diverted the course of the River Tweed to prevent the foundations from being undermined.

Selected Walks in the Southern and Central Highlands and Cairngorms

Rennie McOwan

Glen Coe

INTRODUCTION

Asked to select eight walks of varying lengths in an area south of the Great Glen and more or less to the north of a line between Edinburgh and Glasgow, I was faced with an embarrassment of riches. How could I leave out the linking summits of the Mamores, the main peaks of the Cairngorms, the Monadh Liath, Creag Meaghaidh, Ben Alder and the hills around Loch Ossian and Loch Treig? The same reluctance was evoked by the thought of the round tops of the Drumochter Pass, cone-shaped Schiehallion, the Glen Coe hills, the attractive peaks at Arrochar, the Loch Tay-side and Glen Lyon hills, and many other fine walks.

In an attempt to overcome this near-impossible task I have concentrated on routes which are fulfilling in themselves and which can also provide walkers with an introduction to an area. These walks are both a foretaste and a full meal. Each can be enjoyed for its own sake once its character and status has been identified and appreciated and yet each opens a door to wider horizons.

Scotland has several hills of a near-mystical character, but perhaps none more so than Bennachie, much beloved of north-east folk and with a history which far outweighs its size. It is a tasty morsel on a rich plate. The same is true of Dunchuach, at Inveraray, famous in clan legend. Both of these small hills are ideal for family scrambles or afternoon or evening walks. Ben Nevis has to be included because it is Britain's biggest mountain, but the route includes views of its often hidden and magnificent cliffs.

Two classic Cairngorms passes are chosen: the Lairig Ghru through the main plateau and the Tolmount, which connects Glen Clova and Braemar. Both are rich in tales and legends and offer views to other hills. Both are major walks. The crossing of Rannoch Moor gives a taste of one of the last wildernesses, while the two Glen Coe passes, the Lairig Eilde and the Lairig Gartain, are pleasant walks in themselves, besides serving as an introduction to Glen Coe. The Callander to Glen Dochart hill and pass walk is demanding, but also gives the feel of the softer slopes of the southern Highlands.

All such choices are subjective. But if they make you come back, then that is what they were meant to do. Happy walking!

1.9

DUN NA CUAICHE (DUNCHUACH) HILL, INVERARAY

STARTING AND FINISHING
POINT
Inveraray Castle car-park (56-
095094). Turn off the A83 at
Inveraray town.
LENGTH
2½ miles (4 km)
ASCENT
800 ft (240 m)

This walk and the drive to Inveraray (pronounced *Inver-air-ah*), the old capital of Clan Campbell and home of the Duke of Argyll, give something of the flavour of the fine hills and the turbulent history of what used to be known as 'shire Argile'.

The small hill of Dunchuach (pronounced *Dun-whoo-ich*) overlooking Inveraray Castle, has an almost mystical appeal. It offers fine views down Loch Fyne and to the surrounding hills and glens, as well as to the inlet loch of Loch Shira at its foot. The ascent is made through attractive woodland and there is a circular return. The paths have been discreetly waymarked by the Argyll estates, and the 'blue' route to the summit and back, lasting about 2½–3 hours, is by far the best walk.

ROUTE DESCRIPTION (Map 12)

From the car-park at Inveraray Castle *(1)* follow the estate road across a bridge and the River Aray in a northerly direction. Passing attractive trees, some of them commemorating the visit by Queen Victoria to the castle in 1875, go straight across a field in the direction of large coniferous trees to a green gate. Please shut the gate. You are now in an old arboretum *(2)*. The route continues past the remains of a lime kiln, the product of which was used in past times as fertilizer. It is best to view these buildings from nearby and not to climb over them. A short walk branches off from here, but you continue upwards on the blue route.

Turn sharp R and follow the old road for 25 yards (20 metres) then turn sharp L and proceed up hill. These woods are rich in flowers and insects and there is a wide variety of birds. The woods are particularly attractive in spring when the

Inveraray Castle

bluebells (wild hyacinths) are out. Through a gap in the trees, a tall circular building, a dovecote built in 1748, can be seen in the middle distance *(3)*.

Turn L on the blue route and there is a short section of single-track footpath leading to a level section of the track from which there are good views *(4)*. The path continues in an easterly direction towards Loch Fyne and you soon reach a view-point for the castle, the town and the surrounding area. There is some scree here—rocks broken up by the action of frost and water—and as it can slide easily you should stick carefully to the path.

The route then turns sharply L and goes uphill. The terrain changes from woodland to near-moorland and then to hill, with birches and heather, rushes and grasses. Continue uphill until you pick up the line of an old road to the top. This is known as *Glac a' Bharaille* ('the hollow of the barrel'). Follow this old road to the summit and its folly in the form of a tower *(5)*. Rest and enjoy the view and try to discern the many layers of history which have shaped this landscape *(6)*.

Take the longer, blue route back down by returning to point 15 and then following the signs. (Do not turn R and return the way you came up.) On reaching the first road proceed downhill to the right for about 100 yards (90 m) and then turn sharp L and follow the footpath through the woods. You will pass a seat, known locally as the 'sweetie seat' (a place for courting and sucking sweets, a courting gift in past times), with fine views. Continue along the section known as the 'Grand Approach' to the castle and then leave the road and descend steeply to the River Aray. Follow the track up the river for about 150 yards (140 m) to return to your starting-point.

1 Inveraray Castle

The Campbells of Argyll were mainly winners in Scottish history and supported the House of Hanover against the exiled House of Stuart. It is a sign of their confidence that the present Inveraray Castle was started by Archibald, the 3rd Duke of Argyll, in the middle of the unsuccessful 1745 Jacobite Rising. It was completed by the 5th Duke 40 years later and replaced a fifteenth-century castle. Four white stones in the field near the car-park mark the older fortification. The new castle was designed by Roger Morris and the construction was supervised by William Adam, father of the architects John, Robert and James. It has fine furnishings and memorabilia of Clan Campbell.

View from the Folly Tower to Inveraray Castle

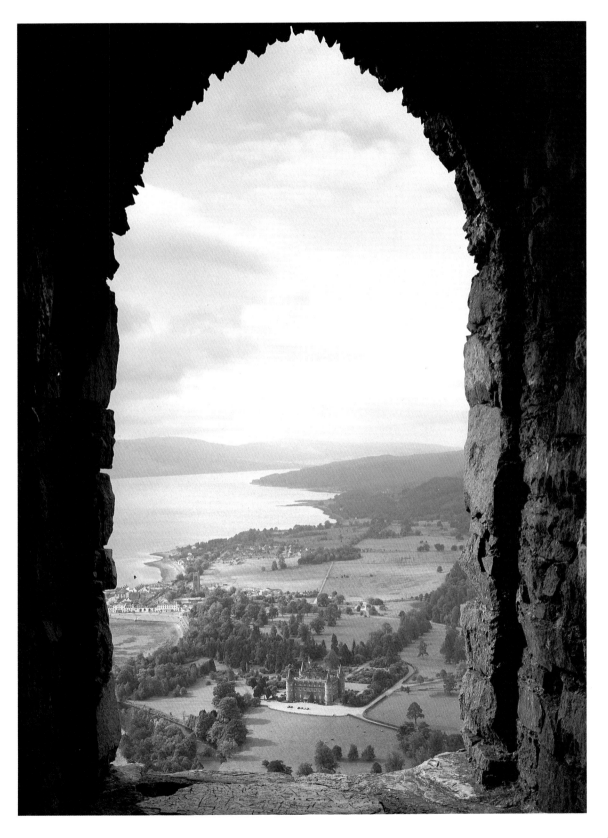

2 The Arboretum

The Argyll family were pioneers in landscaping and forestry as early as the seventeenth century. In this collection of trees are Japanese larch grafted into a European root stock, Japanese cedar, Wellingtonia (named after the Duke of Wellington, who died just before it was 'discovered' in 1841), East Himalayan fir, Algerian fir, western hemlock, grand fir, European silver fir and Japanese yezo or hondo spruce. The Argyll estates produce a booklet identifying the trees.

3 Dovecote

This was built in 1748 as part of the 3rd Duke's plan for his estate. Dovecotes were a common feature of Scottish estates and in earlier centuries Lowland landowners were urged by law to build them; an invader could burn houses and crops and kill or steal livestock, but pigeons were harder to deal with. In the Highlands a lack of feeding led to dovecotes being restricted to owners who could feed the birds, so that neighbours were not troubled. The author Neil Munro made the dovecote a central location in his historical novel *The New Road*, described by John Buchan as the best historical novel since those of Sir Walter Scott. However, the dovecote was built almost thirty years after the 1719 Jacobite Rising.

4 *Views*

As you climb higher you can see how important Dunchuach was to the Campbells as a view-point. Three main glens radiate north from Inveraray—Glen Aray, Glen Fyne and Glen Shira—and Clan Campbell always believed they could block the head of these passes against enemies. And so they could against armies with baggage and cannon. But they were caught out in 1645 in the Scottish Wars of the Covenant when the Royalist army of the Marquis of Montrose and his second-in-command, the war leader of Clan Donald, Alasdair MacColla, sent their fast-moving Gaelic troops through the winter hills. Inveraray was captured and sacked.

5 *The Folly Tower*

This building looks ancient and occurs in Neil Munro's novel, *John Splendid,* when he depicts the Campbell garrison being besieged by Montrose's clansmen. This, alas, was an anachronism—a failing of which Neil Munro was often guilty. The folly is sited so that when seen from the castle and town it is silhouetted against the sky. It was built by Roger Morris and William Adam in 1748 for the then large sum of £46 and was designed to look like a ruin from below.

6 *The Summit*

The name *Dun Na Cuaiche* (Dunchuach) means 'the fort of the cup (or bowl)', probably because of the bowl shape at the top. An Iron Age rampart can also be traced. The neighbouring hill is Duntorvil, a corruption of the Gaelic *Corr-bhile,* meaning 'the (highest) eminence on the ridge'. The wild hill land roundabout is worth scrutiny. Ben Buidhe, ('the yellow mountain') can be seen to the north-east and from the north side of the summit you see one of the great mountains of Scotland, Ben Cruachan (pronounced *Croo-ichin*). In Gaelic this is Cruachan Beann ('the heaped-up hill of the many tops'), the two main summits of which are seen from many parts of the Southern and Central Highlands. Ben Cruachan gave Clan Campbell its war slogan (*'Cruachan!'*) and should be earmarked by all hillwalkers for a future visit. The traverse of

Inveraray Folly

all its peaks makes a fine expedition, but it is a mountain which deserves care and respect. A hydro-electric dam, built between 1961 and 1966, can just be picked out in its central corrie. The hills around Arrochar and Loch Long, Ben Ime and its neighbours, Ben Narnain and the Cobbler, should also be borne in mind for the future.

7 *Rhododendrons*

The shrub was introduced to Britain from Turkey in 1753, and the name means 'the tree of Rhodes from the land on Pontus'. Other varieties come from the Himalayas and the Far East. Its colourful flowers in June bring joy to many, but it is also a problem because it forms dense thickets which block other plants and, unless kept in check, can block paths and forest rides. Argyll's high rainfall and acid soil suit its growth but, unfortunately, it also sours the soil and creates conditions favourable to its own spread.

1.10

BENNACHIE

STARTING AND FINISHING
POINT
Esson's Croft car-park (38-700217)
LENGTH
3¼ miles (5 km)
ASCENT
1200 ft (370 m)

ACCESS
At the village of Kemnay, on the River Don, turn off the B993 on to the Fetternear-Blairdaff road, called Riverside Road. Continue on this road for 2 miles (3 km), then turn R on to the Blairdaff-Chapel of Garioch road. After 1 mile (1.6 km), turn R on to the Chapel of Garioch road. From there drive a further 2 miles (3 km) and find the entrance to the Esson's Croft car-park, marked 'Forest Walks', on the L.

Mither Tap

Bennachie (pronounced *Bain-a-hee*) is one of Scotland's best known mystical hills, a prominent landmark from many parts of Aberdeenshire and dominating the farmlands of the Garioch (pronounced *Gay-ree*) and Buchan. Some historians think that the famous battle of Mons Graupius in AD 84 or 85 took place here. It was then that the invading Romans defeated the Caledonian tribes and their leader Calgacus uttered the famous words: 'They make a desert and they call it peace.'

The Rowan Tree route to the Mither Tap is traditionally the most popular, but it is not the best. That honour belongs to this route, starting at Esson's Croft car-park.

ROUTE DESCRIPTION (Map 13)

From Esson's Croft car-park take the path by the map board, with the toilets on the R. After ¼ mile (400 m), with the Clachie Burn on the L, the path veers R and then L to a fork. Take the L fork and after 50 yards (45 m), turn R at the sign to the Gouk Stone *(1)*. Return to the fork in the track.

Continue for 200 yards (180 m) to where there is a seat and the track branches into three. Take the track to the R and follow it for 200 yards (180 m) out of the trees to Esson's Croft *(2)*. Pass the ruins and after 100 yards (90 m) turn L at the 'T' junction. Continue ahead to the gate and after another 50 yards (45 m) turn R on to the footpath. Follow the path uphill as it meanders out of the trees and on to the summit of 'Mither Tap' *(3)*, a distance of ¾ mile (1.2 km). Near the top the track passes through the outer walls of an Iron Age fort *(4)*. Carefully scramble on to the summit tor, where there is an indicator. This rocky tor is very precipitous on its north and west sides. Return by the same route *(5)*.

1 The Gouk Stone
   Ruined walls in a clearing tell an old and sad story and so does this small standing stone, although it has no markings or

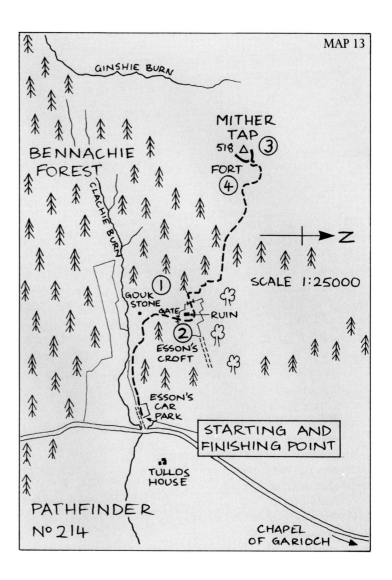

MAP 13

GINSHIE BURN

MITHER
TAP
518 △ ③

BENNACHIE
FOREST

FORT
④

CLACHIE BURN

SCALE 1:25000

GOUK
STONE ①

GATE
② RUIN

ESSON'S
CROFT

ESSON'S
CAR
PARK

STARTING AND
FINISHING POINT

TULLOS
HOUSE

PATHFINDER
No 214

CHAPEL
OF GARIOCH

carvings. It was a marker stone showing the boundary of common land divided by court action in 1859. At the start of the nineteenth century, some tenacious local people, who became known as The Colonists, created crofts for themselves on unpromising land of scrub and heather. Also working as hired help on the bigger farms of the lower ground, they won a living by hard toil and courage. But eight neighbouring estates began a court action in 1844 to divide up the common land between them, and the squatters then became tenants whether they liked it or not. Rent rises over the years eventually forced all the families but one to leave. *Gouk* or *Gowk* is a Scots word for a cuckoo (although it can also mean a fool) and the stone may have been a favourite perching place for this bird in April.

2 Esson's Croft

When the squatters or colonists were squeezed off the land they had won in the face of such adversity, George Esson alone refused to admit defeat. He struggled on and died there in 1938 and the ruins of the croft still bear his name. It is fitting that the car-park at the start of this walk should carry his name, for he deserves to be remembered.

Keep a look out for inscribed stones with initials and nineteenth-century dates. They were erected by the estates which took over the colonists' crofts, to make clear their ownership. One stone is dated '1858', a year in advance of the court's decision. The estate owners must have been very confident of gaining the disputed land.

3 Mither Tap

Bennachie forms a ridge 3 miles (5 km) long, with a series of tops of which the highest is the Oxen (pronounced *Ow-sin*) Craig (1733 ft/528 m). However, the best known and the most attractive summit to ascend is the slightly lower and easternmost point, called the Mither Tap. It is a great cap of granite and although the name is obscure, as is the derivation of Bennachie, it may mean 'the mother-top'. It certainly has

Easter Aquhorthies Stone Circle with Bennachie looming in the distance

something of a matriarchal air about it.

4 *The Fort*

Some authorities say the ancient fort on top of the Mither Tap is a vitrified fort (that is, the walls have been fused by heat and fire) but this is incorrect. Its origins are shadowy, but it is thought to be from between 500 BC and AD 500, the Iron Age. Many tons of stones were brought up the hill to build this fort and within the existing walls were at least ten buildings and a well, now dry.

5 *Return Journey*

This ascent is recommended as an introduction to Bennachie. The views from the Mither Tap and the summit are extensive, to the hills of Caithness, the Cairngorms, around Glen Clova and over the farmlands. It might seem strange to recommend a route which does not go to the summit, but this is a special hill of great character and its qualities cannot be fully appreciated, even on several visits.

2.11

GLEN COE

STARTING AND FINISHING
POINT
Car-parking space in Glen Coe near
The Study waterfall on the A82 to
Fort William (41-189568).
LENGTH
9 miles (14 km)
ASCENT
500 ft (150 m) at the crest of each of
the two passes, the Lairig Eilde and
the Lairig Gartain.

This circular walk goes through two attractive passes running from Glen Coe to Glen Etive and forms a pleasant introduction to the Glen Coe area.

ROUTE DESCRIPTION (Map 14)

The Lairig Eilde (pronounced *Eel-che*) *(1)* to Glen Etive is a right-of-way and is signposted on the south side of the A82 and to the east of the area and waterfall known as The Study. There is room for only a few cars on the north side of the road close to a prominent cairn and to the start of the walk, but further west more parking space can be found. Take great care when walking on the road, one of the busiest in the Highlands.

A tiny path goes over moundy ground on the L (east) side of the burn, the Allt Lairig Eilde, and although it partly continues on this side it is better to cross the burn to the R (west) side where another path is more clearly defined.

On your R (west) are the steep slopes of Beinn Fhada (the second word is pronounced *atta*) the first of the prominent rocky, roadside peaks in Glen Coe known collectively as the Three Sisters. On your L (east) are the slopes of Buachaille Etive Beag *(2)*, a long ridge of a hill which runs from Stob nan Cabar over Stob Coire Raineach to Stob Dubh in the south.

Proceed gradually uphill on a path which has been occasionally cairned, a reprehensible practice *(3)*, with the craggy faces of Stob Coire Sgreamhach, a linked peak to Bidean (pronounced *Bitchen*) nam Bian, the highest mountain in Argyll, half R and starting to dominate the pass. Look out for deer on both sides of the pass at this stage: the area was once a royal hunting forest. There is no problem with deer stalkers: this is National Trust for Scotland ground and, other than a cull, no shooting takes place. The sight and sound of traffic vanishes as you ascend.

At the end of the pass is a cairn and the route then turns due south. Just over the crest of the pass and as you descend to Glen

Etive you will see a prominent, flat-topped stone *(4)* on which a land-boundary deal was signed in clan times. Descend sharply downhill towards the estate lodge of Dalness *(5)*, with good views opening up of lovely Glen Etive. At this point you have a choice of route.

Dalness is private land and was once the reputed site of the legendary Deirdre's bower. It can be viewed only from the hillside and the very nimble need not descend completely to the single-track road which runs past Dalness down Glen Etive and ends at the disused pier at the head of Loch Etive. It is possible to contour the hillside westwards into the return pass, the Lairig Gartain, but this is recommended only for those who are comfortable crossing steep ground. Otherwise, descend to the road where the signposted start of the Lairig Gartain begins and prepare to ascend once again. The Lairig Gartain *(6)* runs north-eastwards from this point on the road.

The pull uphill is steep, but there is a reasonable path which starts to vanish in the upper reaches. It is worth stopping for good views back down Glen Etive to distant Loch Etive and also to see the extent to which modern forestry now cloaks a once-fertile glen *(7)*.

Over the crest of the pass the ground is more featureless, but there is an intermittent path which follows the line of the River Coupall, where there are some fine pools. On your R (east) is the long ridge of that fine mountain the Buachaille Etive Mor *(8)*. Again, keep an eye out for deer. The track reaches the A82 to the west of Lagangarbh mountaineering cottage: be sure to keep on the L (west) side of the River Coupall as you descend. You then walk westwards for about 2 miles (3 km) along the A82 back to your vehicle. Do be careful of cars on this road.

Glen Coe

1 Pass of the Hinds—the Lairig Eilde

The word 'lairig' simply means a pass and the Gaelic word *eilde* means hinds, female deer. It is thus 'the pass of the hinds'. This was a well-used hill crossing from Glen Coe in the past and was possibly used as an escape route by the MacDonalds (MacIains) in the notorious 1692 massacre, although it is about a mile (1.6 km) from the start of the site of the old MacDonald townships and about 4 miles (6.5 km) from where most of the others were sited.

2 *Buachaille Etive Beag*

The little herdsman of Etive, as the name may be translated, shelters the pass on the east and its long ridge comprises three subsidiary peaks. The one nearest the road, Stob nan Cabar, means 'the peak of the *cabar*', the tree-trunk tossed in Highland games, the next (running south-east) is Stob Coire Raineach ('the peak of the ferns or bracken'), and Stob Dubh ('black peak'). Gaelic hill names often give an idea of the terrain.

3 *Cairning*

The National Trust for Scotland's mountaineering benefactor, the late Percy Unna, drew up enlightened rules for the management of hill property. (He also led financial appeals and gave generously himself to enable the Trust to acquire several mountain properties.) These rules included: no man-made structures on the hills, no facilities for food or drink, no new paths to be constructed, the mountains not to be made easier or safer to climb, and no access for wheeled vehicles. His achievements are attracting increasing attention nowa-days as conservation issues reach wider audiences. He detested the cairning of paths and when he found a cairn he kicked it down. Stob Coire Sgreamhach means 'the peak of the rocky corrie'. As a corrie is a kettle—not like the modern handle-and-spout kind, but bowl-shaped—the name indicates a big hollow or saucer-shape in the hills.

4 *Clachan Reamhair*

A cluster of large boulders encountered as you descend from the crest of the pass is known as the Clachan Reamhair ('the traveller's village'). They gave shelter to wanderers. Just before you reach these stones there is a flat stone known as Clach an t-Suidhe ('the stone of the seat'). Campbell of Inverawe signed title deeds of Dalness on this stone in stiff discussions with the MacDonalds of Dalness, whose clanspeople were a sept linked to the MacDonalds (MacIains) of Glen Coe, and who were suspicious of Clan Campbell's expansionist policies.

5 *Dalness*

Now a shooting estate, this was once a Clan Donald holding. Neil Munro brought the house into his historical novel *John Splendid*, telling how a band of Campbell fugitives returning from the battle of Inverlochy in 1645 were almost trapped by the MacDonalds. A gun reputed to have been used in the killing of Colin Campbell of Glen Ure in the period following the 1745 Jacobite Rising was kept at Dalness for a time. Robert Louis Stevenson used this killing, known as the Appin murder, in *Kidnapped*, when Colin Campbell was shot by an unknown sniper while on his way to evict the Stewart tenants who had supported the Jacobites. Stevenson called Colin Campbell the Red Fox and the gun was known as the Black Gun of Misfortune because an innocent man, James Stewart of the Glens, was hanged for the murder. The killer of the Red Fox remains an enduring Scottish mystery.

6 *The Lairig Gartain*

This was another popular hill crossing in past centuries. Seen from the A82, the crest of the pass shows a lovely scallop shape between the two Buachailles. Gartain is a man's name and this whole corner is still known as the Royal Forest of Dalness and marked on the maps as such. Great deer hunts sometimes involved hundreds of men and the deer were driven into enclosures or 'box canyons', called *elrigs*, and then killed by spear, sword and axe. The Dalness area was popular with Scottish kings in past times and much political discussion took place at such hunt gatherings.

7 *Glen Etive*

The glen was once very fertile and supported many townships, but is now given over to hill farming and forestry. The name *etive* derives from a word for an old Celtic storm goddess. Loch Etive is almost 18 miles (29 km) long and is tidal. It is flanked by fine mountains, worth noting for future exploration, including Ben Starav ('the strong mountain') and Ben Trilleachan ('mountain of sandpipers') beloved of slab rock-climbers, but which can also be ascended by walkers from Loch Etive-side. Another fine walk runs down the north shore of Loch Etive to Dail and Cadderlie, a reputed Deirdre bower site (see below), on an island, and where there was once an ancient orchard.

An old Scottish and Irish Gaelic legend tells of Deirdre of the Sorrows and how she and her lover Naoise (pronounced *Noy-sha*) lived a life of Golden Age joy in different parts of the Highlands and had a special haven or bower in Glen Etive. Deirdre was lured by the jealous King Conchobar of Ulster back to Ireland, where she and Naoise were killed. Tribal war broke out as a result, thus fulfilling an ancient prophecy that Naoise's family, the House of Uisnach (pronounced *Wish-na*), would be the cause of the fall of the House of Ulster. Deirdre is regarded as the Celtic Helen and the Gaelic people in centuries past believed the old tale to be true.

8 *Buachaille Etive Mor*

'The great herdsman of Etive' is one of the best-known mountains of Scotland, with its main, sharp-pointed peak, Stob Dearg (pronounced *Stob Jerrack*) ('the red peak') dominating the road from the south. Like its neighbour,

Previous page: *Dalness*
Opposite: *Waterfall below The Study*

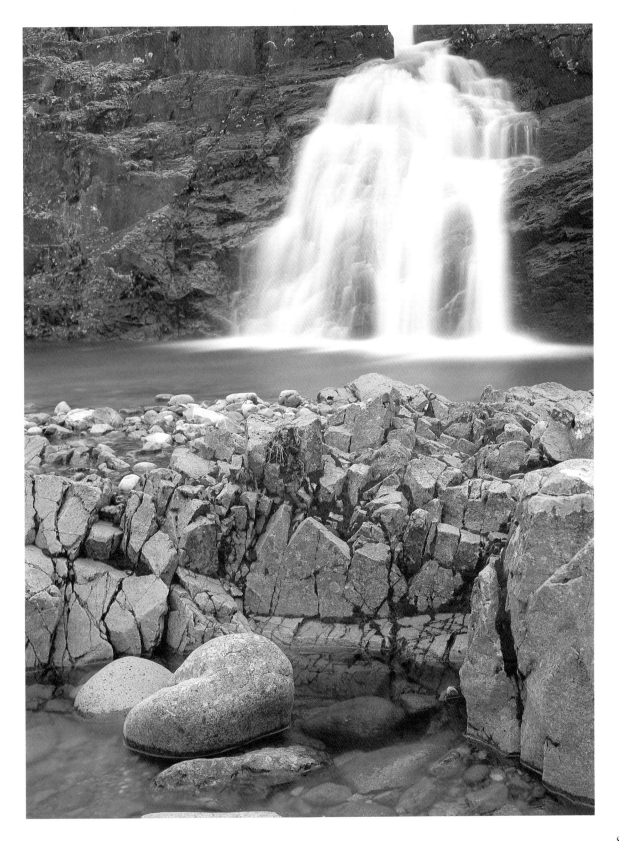

Buachaille Etive Beag, it sends a long ridge running to the south-east and which ends in Stob na Broige ('the peak of the shoe'), from which the word 'brogue' comes. Its steep slopes hide the top peaks when the walker is in the Lairig Gartain, but its closeness, and that of its neighbour, Buachaille Etive Beag, and the views all round from the passes, provide a good introduction to the eastern end of the Glen Coe area.

3.12

THE GREAT MOOR OF RANNOCH

STARTING POINT
There is parking space at Rannoch
Station halt at the west end of the
B846, which runs from
Kinlochrannoch and along the north
side of Loch Rannoch (42-424578).
This road connects on the east with
the B8019 to Killiecrankie and the
main A9 and also runs southwards to
Aberfeldy.
FINISHING POINT
There is parking space at Kingshouse
Hotel (41-261545), just to the east of
the A82 and linked with it by hotel
drives, and ¼ mile (1.2 km) south-
east of the Glen Etive road junction.
LENGTH
13 miles (21 km)
ASCENT
1150 ft (350 m); 2400 ft (730 m) if
the hill of Stob na Cruaiche is
included.

It might seem odd to talk of a wilderness which includes a road, a railway and a line of telephone poles running through it, but it is nevertheless true of the Great Moor of Rannoch. Its peat hags, heather mounds, small lochans, burns and infant rivers cover over 56 sq miles (145 sq km). It is a haven for many deer and cackling grouse, while goosanders and black- and red-throated divers can be seen on its many lochans. The going is often rough and it should be undertaken only by a fit party accustomed to outdoor navigation.

ROUTE DESCRIPTION (Maps 15, 16)

Cross the north-south Glasgow to Fort William railway line through an official gate and just to the south of the rail halt itself (1). A sign outlines the route's right-of-way status. Proceed north-west on a broad track for about ¼ mile (400 m) with the Dubh Lochan ('the small black loch') on your L (west) and follow this track until it curves north and then south-west alongside modern forestry plantations. The OS map shows a path, but it frequently vanishes and this section of the walk between the trees and the tiny, golden beaches of Loch Laidon is often boggy and wet because of drainage from these plantations. Sometimes there is nothing to do but grimace and splash on through intermittent birch and alder trees. Walking on the sands is not really an assured alternative because they, too, are often soggy.

Continue south-west along the north shore of Loch Laidon until you are clear of the trees. In summer, and in fine weather, some walkers temporarily deviate from the route and climb north-westwards to the top of Stob na Cruaiche ('the heaped-up peak') which gives magnificent views of the moor's sea-like appearance (2). The going on the hill is heavy—allow at least an hour. During the stag-shooting season, 1 July to 20 October,

give this hill a miss and stick to the right-of-way route.

The path vanishes, but the trees of the little island, Eilean Iubhair ('island of the yews') show up ahead *(3)* and just north of the island are the ruins of Tigh na Cruaiche ('the house of the heaped-up place'). This is surrounded by pleasant green grass in marked contrast to the heather and the peat hags of the rest of the moor. If you want to include Stob na Cruaiche, descend directly to this ruin. There are the remains of two buildings here, an old sheep pen and cottage and a little bothy, fast becoming ruinous. People have slept in these, but they should now be treated as no more than windbreaks. The spot makes a pleasant resting place.

The path continues westwards and frequently vanishes, and three major burns have to be crossed. The remains of old tree roots may be visible in the peat-bog. You may have to cast up and down the banks of the burns to find a crossing place if there has been a lot of rain recently, which is a probability, but there should be no major difficulty.

A line of telephone poles is picked up over the brow of the moor and should be followed until a broad, man-made track is reached just to the east of Allt Dubh Mor ('the big black burn').

Follow this track westwards until it reaches the shooting lodge at Black Corries. The higher ground here gives evocative views back over some of the lower ground you have traversed. Follow this track westwards for another 2½ miles (4 km) until a junction track goes L (south) and reaches Kingshouse Hotel *(4)*. This latter track joins part of the West Highland Way *(5)*.

1 The West Highland Railway
This track was a great feat of the Victorian engineers, who floated the rails on huge rafts of tree roots, brushwood, rock and tons of ashes. They chose a route which the famous engineer Thomas Telford hoped, in vain, would be a road. In January 1889 a group of seven—three civil engineers, the head of the firm of contractors, two estate factors and a solicitor—set out to obtain more information about the railway's probable route. Only one had been on the moor before. They were ill-equipped and one carried an umbrella. They became separated on the moor in mist and totally lost. One found a fence and followed it to the old shepherd's house at Gorton, not far from Auchallader Farm and to the north of Bridge of Orchy, and a search was launched. Amazingly, all were found. That night a severe blizzard broke over the area. They were truly fortunate men.

The peat-hags on Rannoch Moor

2 Rannoch Moor

The name Rannoch is said to come from a Gaelic word for bracken, *ruineach,* although *ratheanach,* watery, seems more likely. Once it was ice-covered and then became a shallow, blanket bog. Much of it was later covered by Scots pines, most of which were cut for ship timber or burned to flush out fugitives in power struggles. The Breadalbane Campbells, who created a few fugitives themselves, spoke of 'Rannoch Muir. . . that thorofare of thieves'.

Many walkers comment on the sea-like appearance of the moor, and the undulating nature of the ground appears deceptively flat from a distance. But it is deceptive, so allow rather more than Naismith's prescribed 3 miles (5 km) an hour when crossing the moor. There is a lot of upping-and-downing. The elk, beaver, northern lynx, caribou, boar, wolf, mosquito and brown bear once had their homes here and people in past times considered it a fearsome place. The nineteenth-century mineralogist, geological surveyor and writer, Dr John Macculloch, said even the crows shunned it (untrue) and he told Sir Walter Scott it was 'a land of desolation and grey darkness'. Neil Munro describes the hero, Aeneas MacMaster, of his historical novel *The New Road* as finding the moor 'the oddest thing, the eeriest in nature he had ever seen'. As readers of *Kidnapped* will know, Robert Louis Stevenson portrayed the dragoons searching the moor for Alan Breck Stewart and David Balfour, an unlikely scenario since most of the terrain would be hard going for cavalry horses.

Much of the moor is privately owned and is designated a Site of Special Scientific Interest, as is Loch Laidon. The moor includes a national nature reserve owned by the Nature Conservancy Council and is rich in botanical interest.

3 Eilean Iubhair

The voracity of sheep and deer, the water-soaked ground, and changes in climate have all contributed to the non-regeneration of trees on Rannoch Moor. The old Caledonian pine forests once covered much of the Highlands and may have given us the alternative name for Scotland, Caledonia, a corruption of Gaelic words meaning a wooded stronghold. Yew trees have flourished on the small island because it has been relatively free of deer and sheep (although deer, of course, can swim long distances if they have to). The origin of the name Laidon is obscure, but it may derive from words for a secure place.

Rannoch Moor near Loch Laidon

4 Kingshouse Hotel

This hostelry claims to be the oldest in Scotland and dates back to the seventeenth century. It was once a military barracks, hence the name King's House, and also a place where coaches changed their tired horses and a place for the Royal Mail. It was also a drover's inn, a halt for the huge cattle drives of last century, when thousands of beasts were driven south from the Highlands and Islands to be sold at the big fairs at Falkirk and Crieff and further south into England. Nowadays it is a mecca for mountaineers and skiers.

5 *The West Highland Way*

This official Long Distance Footpath runs 95 miles (150 km) from Milngavie, near Glasgow, to Fort William and was opened in October 1980. It descends to Kingshouse from a route which fringes Rannoch Moor to the south and then continues from Altnafeadh over to Kinlochleven by the old military road, the Devil's Staircase.

Rannoch Moor at Lochan Gaineamhach

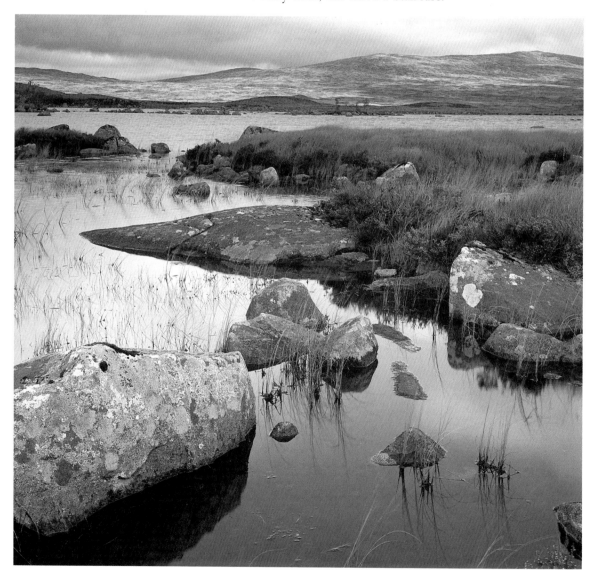

3.13

BEN NEVIS

STARTING AND FINISHING
POINT
Achintee Farm car-park on the minor
road which leads from the Claggan
area of Fort William (41-125731).
Claggan village lies to the north-west
of Fort William on the north bank of
the River Nevis. The road to Achintee
passes through it and runs alongside
the river. The farm is ¾ mile (1.2 km)
south-east of the A82.
LENGTH
12 miles (19 km)
ASCENT
4400 ft (1340 m)

SAFETY NOTE

The mountain is ascended by
thousands of visitors each year, but it
is to be undertaken with care. More
people have been killed on the Ben
than have died on the North Face of
the Eiger. If the hill is snow-plastered,
it should be left to the experienced
climber with axe and crampons.

Some groups climb the Ben by way
of the northern side, following the
line of the Allt a' Mhuilinn burn
above Fort William golf course to the
CIC hut and then on to the arête, but
this route is very eroded in sections
and some people find the climb to the
arête hard and tricky. A direct ascent
(and descent) can be made on the
southern face, from the car-park at
the head of Glen Nevis, but this route
is highly dangerous and is for none
but the most experienced.

Ben Nevis (affectionately referred to as the 'Ben'), Britain's
highest mountain, looks an unspectacular lump from many
places, its bulk dominating the town of Fort William and Loch
Linnhe. But its huge cliffs, more than 1500 ft (460 m) high, are
mainly hidden when the walker is in the town. On sunny and
clear days in summer the views over Lochaber and much of the
central, western and southern Highlands can be immense. (Note
that the Ben has *two* outlier peaks both called Carn Dearg and
not to be confused with Carn Mor Dearg.)

ROUTE DESCRIPTION (Map 17)

The road to Achintee from Claggan passes the town park just
past the houses, the site of the annual Ben Nevis race *(1)* to the
summit and back. On the R is the Roaring Mill in the River
Nevis, a series of pools and cascades, popular with bathers and
fishermen. A good path starts from Achintee. Cross a stile and
the path leads round the shoulder of Meall an t-Suidhe *(2)* and
the upper reaches of Glen Nevis come into sight *(3)*. At about
500 ft (150 m) a junction path from the Glen Nevis Youth
Hostel comes in on your R.

This path forms part of a specially constructed pony trail to a
weather observatory which was sited on the top of Ben Nevis
last century *(4)*. It was also used in a pioneering motoring bid in
which a Model T Ford was driven to the summit *(5)*. The
modern paths, both the main route and the junction path from
the Youth Hostel, are now very eroded and repair work has
been carried out in modern times. You pass the first zig-zags and
cross two aluminium bridges constructed by the Lochaber
mountain-rescue team and at about 1200 ft (370 m) the path
turns north and climbs up a steep score, or gully, in which there
are some rowans and birches.

Walkers going straight to the summit by the main track
should simply continue uphill on the tourist track and will soon
reach the half-way mark at the Red Burn. Care is needed when

the path zig-zags near the precipice. Those taking the following route, intended for those who are nimble on the hill, should continue round to the L by the Lochan Meal an t-Suidhe *(6)*. The lochan is a good spot for a rest. To get into Coire Leis go L on a boggy path which descends a little and then runs north for about ½ mile (800 m) and then curves round to the R, west, and eventually south-east.

The Allt a' Mhuilin ('burn of the mill') is on your L and runs up into the corrie. The ground is often boggy and you pick up the remains of an old deer fence. A path and eroded ground take you round to the CIC hut *(7)*, about 1¼ miles (2 km) from Lochan Meall an t-Suidhe. Cross to the other (east) side of the corrie and steep, rocky and scree-strewn slopes take you to the top of Carn Mor Dearg. The going is rough and the rocks are often loose, but a careful way can be picked to the top *(8)*.

Continue on the obvious arête (ridge), which links with the summit slopes of Ben Nevis, proceeding south and then south-west. The distance is under a mile (1.6 km), but care and time are needed because some rock scrambling is involved and sections of the arête seem narrow to the inexperienced and the pull up the final slopes of the Ben can be tiring. The summit is unmistakable, with the Observatory ruins *(9)* and the Ordnance Survey obelisk. The views can be spectacular.

If you have ascended the whole way by the main tourist track and are tempted to continue to Carn Mor Dearg by descending to the arête, *don't* unless the day is clear and fine and you know what you are about. There have been several accidents here, including five deaths in one incident, and warning poles have been erected. Take care, too, on the edges of the plateau, particularly if snow is still around. The summit plateau stretches to about 90 acres (36.5 hectares), but take care on the edges. As you leave the Observatory ruins and the OS indicator you pass quite close to the brink of the cliffs of the north face. The path here is safe, but exercise caution nonetheless.

To descend, pick up the zig-zags of the well-cairned tourist track to the west of the summit and follow these down to the junction at Lochan Meall an t-Suidhe. Look out for a 'well' at about 3500 ft (1070 m) which emerges from beneath the stones. It is known as Buchan's Well and is named after a former secretary of the Scottish Meteorological Society.

1 Ben Nevis Race
This famous race, regarded as one of the hardest in Britain, began in 1895, and there are accounts from before it reached

View south from the Ben Nevis tourist path

its current formalized state, of young and old clocking up some remarkable times. A Mr D. Forbes, of Fort William, reached the summit in three hours and danced a Highland fling on the roof of the observatory there. He was 80. The race was discontinued when the observatory closed in 1904 and also perhaps because in 1903 a contestant had collapsed and remained unconscious for ten hours.

In 1937 the race began again but was temporarily halted once more when World War II broke out. It was resumed in 1943. The number of runners has now soared to more than 500 and the event is still sometimes hit by fierce summit weather. Dave Cannon, of Kendal Athletic Club, won five times in the 1970s and clocked 1 hour 26 minutes and 55 seconds. Women were first officially accepted in 1981. The race is normally held on the first Saturday in September.

2 *Meall an t-Suidhe*

The name of this hill (pronounced *mowl-an-tee)* is translated as 'the moundy hill of the seat'. Above it and the lochan (small loch) of the same name is the half-way point on the tourist track. Just beyond, there was a hut where walkers were charged one shilling for a ticket entitling them to walk to the top. When they got there, they had their ticket stamped with the words 'Ben Nevis Summit'. The receipts were used to keep the path in good condition.

3 *Glen Nevis*

An old tradition has it that the Camerons of Glen Nevis held their lands by the tenure of an unfailing snowball when demanded. There is a similar Highland tradition about the MacIntyres of Glen Noe, Argyll, and Ben Cruachan, the Munros of Foulis and Ben Wyvis, and the Grants of Rothiemurchus and the Cairngorms. Deep pockets of snow, of course, lie on Ben Nevis all year round and in past times they were dug out for curing fish and taken down in panniers by horses.

Glen Nevis is a beautiful glen and was once the home of the MacSorleys and MacMillans, as well as the Camerons. The striking gorge at its head, which leads through to the grassy meadows at Steall (pronounced *stowl)* was the subject of a public outcry when the North of Scotland Hydroelectricity Board earmarked it for a dam. The scheme was later shelved but could be resurrected.

4 *Observatory*

The meteorological observatory and hotel were built on the summit last century. The observatory was proposed in 1877 by Mr Milne Home, chairman of the Scottish Meteorological Society, but before it was built readings were first taken in

1881 by the scientist Clement L. Wragge, who was later to become Government Meteorologist for Queensland, Australia.

The first observatory was a sheet of tarpaulin covering a stone hut and then a proper building was erected, with sleeping and cooking facilities, and was operated for twenty-one years. It was the first mountain-top observatory in Europe and was officially opened on 17 October 1883. It was linked by phone and telegraph to the post office at Fort William and a hotelier of that town later built a wooden 'hotel' nearby for walkers who wanted to see the sun rise.

Visiting student staff included C. T. R. Wilson, who won the Nobel prize for the development of nuclear physics. The optical phenomena occurring when the sun shone on the clouds influenced his thoughts towards imitating them in the laboratory, which led to forty years of tracking atoms. Lack of finance closed the observatory for good on 1 October 1904, but the 'hotel' lingered on until World War I. Modern walkers should reflect that the Ben's winter temperatures are similar to those of Arctic Norway, that there is an average of over 200 gales a year, and that the mountain is top of the 'wind-chill' league.

5 *Ascent by car*

A 20-horse-power Model T Ford was driven to the summit as a publicity stunt in 1911 by Henry Alexander, Jr, the son of the owner of Alexander, the Ford agents in Edinburgh. Ten days were spent researching a route and bridging planks were carried. Three more days were spent in driving the car to the half-way mark and two more to reach the observatory. Three times the car was pulled out by rope from boggy ground. The descent took two hours, pipers headed a triumphal procession through the town, and a public holiday was declared. The feat was repeated by Mr Alexander in 1928, this time driving a Model A Ford touring car. He took one day, and the last ¼ mile (400 m) was driven with four passengers in addition to the driver.

6 *Lochan Meall an t-Suidhe*

See note 2. Coire Leis (pronounced *'laish'*) means 'the corrie (hollow) of the sheltered place'.

7 *The CIC Hut*

This Alpine-style, small, stone building at 2200 ft (670 m) is not an open hostel and is owned by the Scottish Mountaineering Club. Dr and Mrs William Inglis Clark donated the hut in memory of their son, Captain Charles Inglis Clark, himself a climber of note, who was killed in World War I. The hut was opened in 1929.

Ben Nevis from Corpach

A hut dinner was held to celebrate the opening and the blessing was given by the Rev. A. E. Robertson, the first man to climb all the 'Munros'. Mr Robertson prayed the building might be a refuge to those in need. He had a dramatic response. In burst two climbers who had fallen 600 ft (180 m) down Observatory Gully, shaken and bruised.

8   *The Nevis Cliffs*

The main climbs on this north-east face of the Ben, when seen from the slopes of Carn Mor Dearg, include (from the right), the prow of Castle Ridge and the buttresses and gullies of the Castles. Then comes the summit of Carn Dearg itself which is flanked to its left by a wide gully, Moonlight Gully. A three-pronged buttress (L) is known as the Trident and it, in turn, is flanked by two gullies near the line of the summit plateau, No. 4 Gully and No. 3 Gully. Then comes the long line of Tower Ridge running from the plateau down into the corrie and then the on-facing North-east Ridge which is flanked to its left by Observatory Ridge and the arête. All of these features are interspersed by rock, snow and ice climbs of all grades.

9   *The summit*

There has been controversy in modern times over the true height of the Ben and 4418 ft (1350 m) has been given. This includes the OS obelisk, and so the true height is 12 ft (3.7 m) less. The Ben is very busy in season and the monuments on top include memorials to the dead of two world wars and the victims of Hiroshima.

Ben Wyvis and the Cairngorms, to the north-north-east and the east, are almost 60 miles (95 km) away, but can be picked out, as can nearer peaks such as Schiehallion at Loch Rannoch, Ben More and Stobinian at Crianlarich, Buachaille Etive Mor in Glen Coe, Beinn Laoigh (Lui) at Tyndrum, and the Arrochar hills. Southwards and westwards one can see the islands, Arran and Jura, Colonsay, Lismore and Mull and far-off Coll and Tiree. Further still are Barra and South Uist in the Outer Hebrides, over 90 miles (145 km) away and these are seen beyond the smaller Rum, Eigg and Canna.

The Cuillin of Skye can also be seen beyond the hills known as the Streaps, near Loch Arkaig, and to the north-west are Ben Sgriol, across from Knoydart, the Kintail Hills, Torridon, and those fine hills above Glen Affric, Mam Sodhail and Carn Eige. On very clear days the line of the sea can be seen beyond Jura and sometimes a far, low line of land can be picked out: the coast of Northern Ireland, over 120 miles (195 km) away. Nearer at hand, lie the hills, glens and lochs of Lochaber and the Mamores just across the glen.

Summit of Mither Tap

THE TOLMOUNT AND JOCK'S ROAD

STARTING POINT
The foot of Red Craig, on the north side of the road at Braedownie Farm, Glen Clova (44-288757), Angus.
FINISHING POINT
Auchallater Farm, 1¼ miles (3 km) south of Braemar on the A93 (43-155884).
LENGTH
13 miles (21 km)
ASCENT
3000 ft (900 m) at the crest of the pass.

SAFETY NOTE
This is a walk to be undertaken with care, with full hill gear, a map and a compass and the ability to use both. It is one of the most evocative hill passes in Scotland, but it is not to be trifled with.

ACCESS
To get to the head of Glen Clova, drive on the B965 from Kirriemuir, in Angus, and follow the line of the glen on the west side until you reach the inn at Clova, where there is a bridge over the River South Esk. Continue westwards on a smaller road for 2¼ miles (3.5 km) until you reach the road-end near Braedownie (pro-nounced *Braedoonie*) farm. There is some parking space in a quarry on the R (north) side of the road at the foot of Red Craig and an official Forestry Commission site further on.

This historic hill crossing leads from Glen Clova into Glen Doll and crosses a plateau of high hills. It is a walk of contrasts: green Glen Clova and dark Glen Doll, the tiny path leading uphill beside a hill burn to the plateau; big, near-featureless hills and magnificent views; and then a steep drop down to Loch Callater and an onwards, straightforward walk to the A93 in Glen Clunie, and on into Braemar.

ROUTE DESCRIPTION (Maps 18, 19)

The start of the Jock's Road and Tolmount walk is signposted, as is another pass which comes in from the north near Braedownie, the Capel Mount *(1)* leading to Ballater.

Walk along the road past Glen Doll Youth Hostel and continue on an estate track and path through forestry plantations. Be sure to stay on the R (north) side of the burn, as it is tempting at one stage to go southwards at a junction. The path becomes clearer as it continues westwards and upwards through the trees, some of them showing the result of storms of past years, until it emerges on the open hillside, surrounded by steep and rocky hills. The White Water burn is prominent ahead and on the L, and the path starts to go steeply uphill on the R. This uphill section in Glen Doll is the true Jock's Road *(2)*. Keep going uphill and watch out on the L for a tiny mountain shelter not far from the head of the pass, just to the west of Cairn Lunkard and known as Dave's Bourach *(3)*.

Nearby and on the R of the path is a plaque on a boulder commemorating five hillwalkers who died in storms on the plateau at New Year 1959 *(4)*. The path proceeds north-west with the Munro–top of Tom Buidhe on the L, the Tolmount peak half–L ahead and Cairn Bannoch and its outliers to the R. This is the crux of the pass. Some walkers make deviations to walk to the summit of one or all of these hills and then return to the pass route. If you do deviate, make sure that you have plenty of time. There is a gradual climb to the summit of the pass at 3,000 ft (900 m).

It is easy to lose the path on this part of the crossing and on the central plateau it is often non-existent, but the positions of Tolmount and Tom Buidhe provide an excellent guide to the route. Keep the burn on the east side of Tom Buidhe to your L and proceed over the mound known as Crow Craigies.

From the summit of the pass you can look to the main Cairngorms plateau, north-eastwards over Broad Cairn towards the royal mountain of Lochnagar, and south-westwards to the hills around Glen Shee.

The Tolmount itself shields the steep head of Glen Callater and the path swings westwards below the Knaps of Fafernie and Creag Leachdach, passing through a shallow dip and beside an old fence, and goes steeply down into Coire Breac (not on the map).

The descent to the east of lonely Loch Kander and the Kander Corrie is steep and broken up and you come across the remains of old fence poles. But Loch Callater ahead is an excellent marker and a small burn is picked up, the path going down its east bank and past some shieling ruins *(5)*. Some of the ground is boggy. Continue on the east side of the loch. If by some chance you cross the burn, the Allt an Loch, to the west side there is also a broad track down that side of the loch to its northern end, where there is a lodge. This broad estate-road running down Glen Callater and below Creag Phadruig *(6)* reaches the A93 at Auchallater in Glen Clunie. There is room for parking there, but some walkers prefer to walk another 1¾ miles (3 km) on into Braemar. Be careful of traffic and walk on the R-hand side of the road, facing oncoming vehicles.

1 The Tolmount

This truly historic pass includes Jock's Road and connects Glen Clova with Deeside. It is one of several of similar character in this area. The old name of the Grampians was the Mounth, which derived from the Gaelic *monadh,* meaning a mountain area or high moorland. The old name for the Cairngorms was the Monadh Rhuadh ('red') and we still have the Monadh Liath ('grey').

The word was corrupted to the Mounth and later came to be applied to individual hill passes and to describe the hill ground as a whole between Upper Deeside and the low ground of Perthshire and west Angus. The correct name of the pass which includes Jock's Road is the Tolmount or Tolmounth. 'Tol' probably derives from a Gaelic word *dail,*

*Previous page: Jock's Road looking towards
Glen Doll*

meaning a meadow or flat place, as around Braedownie and in fertile Glen Clova.

2 *Jock's Road*

This Glen Doll pass is a right-of-way and was the subject of a a much-publicized nineteenth-century court case. In 1888 a Scot called Duncan Macpherson, who had made his wealth in Australia, bought the Glen Doll estate and tried to close it to the public. The Scottish Rights of Way Society fought him and won, proving that the pass had been a 'trade route' over the years.

The case ultimately went to the House of Lords. A witness and shepherd called James Winter, from Braedownie, said in evidence that the name Jock's Road derived from a land dispute between two owners, Lord Aberdeen and Lord Invercauld. The witness said he was descended from one John Winter, who was allegedly involved with others in forcing Lord Aberdeen to turn back when they met him on the track. Lord Aberdeen was incensed and offered a reward for anyone who could name the ringleader. John Winter felt it prudent to take refuge for some time at the top of Glen Doll in a shepherd's hut and that, said James Winter, was the derivation of Jock's Road.

Looking towards Cairn Lunkard

MAP 19

BRAEMAR
1 3/4 miles

A93

FINISHING
POINT

AUCHALLATER

GLEN CLUNIE

CALLATER BURN

N

600

600

708 CREAG
⑥ PHADRUIG

849

800

834
800

GLEN CALLATER

LOCH
CALLATER

ALLT AN LOCH

800

900

800

LANDRANGER
Nº43 AND Nº44

⑤

GLEN CALLATER

LOCH
KANDER

CREAG
LEACHDACH

SCALE 1:50000

CONTINUED
FROM MAP 18

3 Mountain shelter

This little stone hut to the L of the path is informally called Dave's Bourach after Davy Glen, a modern man-of-the-road, and it may be on the site of the original Jock's refuge.

4 The plaque

If you walk this pass on a sunny and clear day, it is all too easy to scoff at the mention of safety. But it is a different matter when the plateau is shrouded in mist or plastered in soft and deep snow, and gales are battering the energy from you. The walkers commemorated by the plaque were from Glasgow Universal Hiking Club and included highly experienced people. They were travelling from Braemar to Glen Doll and lost their way in stormy weather on the plateau between the Tolmount and the start of the Jock's Road section. One body was found a few hundred yards from this shelter, then a mainly wooden hut. Some bodies were not found until weeks later. Another couple died in similar storms in March 1976.

5 Shielings

The Gaelic people in past centuries left their homes in late spring and headed with their cattle and goats for the fresh grass of the upper glens and moors. They lived in makeshift huts called shielings and returned to the lower ground at the end of summer.

6 Creag Phadruig

This crag and a loch nearby take their name from a legendary priest called Patrick (whose name is also commemorated in Carn an t-Sagairt Mor (pronounced *Carn Tagart More*), a peak on the route from Loch Callater to the royal mountain of Lochnagar. (Earmark both Carn an t-Sagairt Mor and Lochnagar for another expedition.) A local tradition has it that when the district experienced what seemed like everlasting frosts they called on Patrick for help. He went to a holy well near Loch Callater and prayed until the ice melted. Rain clouds gathered over Carn an t-Sagairt Mor and the thaw began. The old Gaelic people have nearly all gone from these areas but their names and legends still linger in these hills and add to their charm.

The White Water above Glen Doll

4.15

THE LAIRIG GHRU

STARTING POINT
Entrance gate to Glen Lui, ¼ mile
(400 m) east of Linn of Dee and on
the left of the minor road which runs
westwards for 5 miles (8 km) from
Braemar (off A93) and then curves
eastwards across the River Dee at
Linn of Dee (43-068899).
FINISHING POINT
Coylum Bridge village on the A951, 2
miles (3 km) from Aviemore (A9)
(35-918107)
LENGTH
17 miles (27 km)
ASCENT
2750 ft (840 m) at the crest of the
pass.

SAFETY NOTE
Full hill gear should be carried: people
have died in this pass and particular
care is needed in spring and winter.

The spectacular gash of the Lairig Ghru through the Cairngorms plateau is a route of great antiquity, packed with legend, an evocative introduction to the area, and one of the best cross-country treks in Scotland.

The crossing is made by thousands each year and sections of the path are now eroded. It is a very old right-of-way and was once much used by the people of Mar and Upper Strathspey.

ROUTE DESCRIPTION (Maps 20–23)

There is parking space on the L of the road at Linn of Dee and just before the entrance to Glen Lui. The Water of Lui burn is on your R as you pass through a gate on your L on to a broad, stony track. Proceed on this for just over a mile (1.6 km) and as you clear a wood there is a bridge across Lui Water *(1)*. Continue north-west on this track for another 1½ miles (2.5 km) until you reach a boarded-up (at the time of writing) house (R), called Derry Lodge *(2)*. Go past the lodge and through the trees until the ground is more open. Another glen, Glen Derry, and its burn, comes in from the north (R) and on your L is another cottage, Luibeg *(3)*. The Lairig Ghru is signposted at this point and you cross the Derry burn by a bridge and proceed westwards into Glen Luibeg and through groves of attractive pine trees.

About ½ mile (800 m) to the west of Derry Lodge the large track ends just clear of the trees and a path is picked up. A copse of trees here is known as Preas nam Meirleach, the Robbers' Copse *(4)*. The path is then crossed by another burn coming in from the north, the Luibeg burn, and you can either wade it at this point or, if the water is high, go up the east bank of the burn for under ¼ mile (400 m), to a bridge.

Turn southwards again to the main track and continue westwards for 2 miles (3 km). Curve north-westwards and then north, on a clear path into Glen Dee, the wide glen of the River Dee. You pass below Carn a' Mhaim (R) and there should be

good views to the steep, rocky slabs of The Devil's Point *(5)*, half-L ahead, and attractive Glen Geusachan on your L. You are now into the main line of the Lairig Ghru and on the L (west) side of the path and on the L (west) bank of the River Dee you should see a small, stone bothy with a 'tin' roof. This is the famous Corrour Bothy, a much-loved place in Cairngorms lore *(6)*. A very eroded path leads down to a bridge and an even more eroded one to the bothy itself, which is spartan and unlocked. It is a good place for a halt or a refuge in bad weather.

Return to the path and after about ¼ mile (400 m) look out for a large boulder at the R side of the path. This is Clach nan Tailer ('the stone of the tailors') *(7)* which figured in a Cairngorms story of hill storms and tragedy. Continue northwards on the path below the slopes of Cairn Toul (L) and Ben Macdui (R) and look out on your L for the magnificent Garbh Coire ('the rough corrie') *(8)*. The path becomes increasingly stony and begins to rise to its crest. Boulder fields make for some awkward walking, particularly in new snow, and 3 miles (5 km) from Corrour the crest is reached and marked by small lochans, the Pools of Dee *(9)*. Continue to the L of these. The boulder fields continue for about a mile (1.6 km) and the track is sometimes lost among them.

The route goes downhill and passes below Creag an Leth-Choin (Lurcher's Crag). About 2½ miles (4 km) from the Pools of Dee another junction path goes off R (north-east) to Glen More and the foot of Cairngorm. Continue downhill on the R (east) bank of the burn and you pass a modern building, the Sinclair Memorial Hut *(10)* (L) on the other bank. Stay on the R (east) side of the burn, the Allt Druidh, as you descend. The path downhill reaches the lovely woods of Rothiemurchus south of this hut and you pass between the lower slopes of Cairn Eilrig

Previous page: *Looking across Loch Morlich towards Lairig Ghru and the Cairngorm range*

(L) and Castle Hill on your R (east). Ignore a junction path going right (east). Descend steeply on a good path through these attractive woods for another mile (1.6 km) until you come to a path junction. Go L (west).

After 1¼ miles (2 km) you reach the Cairngorm Club's footbridge *(11)* across the now-enlarged Alt Druidh burn which has been joined by the Am Beanaidh from the south. Just after the footbridge you come to another junction path coming in from the L (west). Continue straight on downhill and about 1½ miles (2.5 km) from the bridge another junction path comes in from the south, down from Gleann Einich. Continue northwards through trees for another ½ mile (800 m) and you reach the road near a caravan park at Coylum Bridge, where there is a hotel ¼ mile (400 m) L (west).

1 Lui Water

The name 'Lui' derives from the Gaelic *laoigh*, a calf, and in most cases where it occurs means a deer calf. Another famous Cairngorm pass, the Lairig an Laoigh, links with the Lairig Ghru just past Derry Lodge and in past times cattle were often driven through it. Cattle and sheep were driven through the Lairig Ghru, too, and Highland girls once walked through the pass in summer carrying baskets of eggs on their heads.

2 Derry Lodge

This building is a relic of the heyday of stag shooting. The name derives from the Gaelic *doire*, meaning a grove or clump of trees. That peerless naturalist, piper, hillwalker and writer Seton Gordon, who died in 1977, recalled playing golf in the clearing between the trees at Derry Lodge with a famous stalker, old Donald Fraser, but all traces of the home-made 'course' have now gone.

3 Luibeg

This name means 'the little calf'. The keeper's house here is one of the few remaining buildings in a glen and strath which once held dozens of houses. The ruins or foundations of some can be seen on the left beside the track between Linn of Dee and Derry Lodge. Some of those expelled to make way for the big sporting estates of the nineteenth century were the descendants of people who had fought on the Jacobite side in the 1715 rising and some of them were evicted not long after that time. The two main passes of the Cairngorms diverge at this point, the Lairig Laoigh going north by Glen Derry, the Lairig Ghru west by Glen Luibeg.

4 Preas nam Meirleach

This grove of trees on the outermost fringe of the pines as you proceed westwards is reputed to be a place where cattle raiders from Lochaber hid from possible pursuit. A burn of that name joins the Luibeg burn just over a mile (1.6 km) to the west of Derry Lodge. The path passes below a hill site which has a legend of buried treasure attached to it, Coire Craobh an Oir, on the hill called Carn Crom.

The hill's name means a twist or bend and a coire (corrie) is a saucer- or bowl-shaped depression in the hills (long ago, the word meant a kettle or cauldron).

5 The Devil's Point

This name is a polite or coy interpretation of the original Gaelic name Bon au Deamhain (pronounced *Pote an dyaw-in*), 'the Devil's penis'. Nearly all Gaelic names are descriptive and often give valuable information about the state of the ground. At this point you are passing below the slopes of

The woods of Rothiemurchus near the Cairngorm Club's footbridge

Carn a' Mhaim (the last word is pronouned *vane*), 'the middle cairn', and looking across to the mass of Beinn Bhrotain (pronounced *pain vroetan*).

This hill derives its name from Brodan, the dog of Fingal, the hero-king of Gaelic mythology (although he may have had a factual basis). There are good views into magnificent Glen Geusachan, 'the glen of the little pine wood'. The name derives from Giubhsachain (pronounced *gyoosachan*). The pines have now gone and only stumps remain, but one of the joys of the Lairig Ghru crossing is that it gives such good views to so many striking mountains and big corries which can be borne in mind for the future.

6 *Corrour Bothy*

This is perhaps the most famous mountain shelter in the Cairngorms. The name derives from the wide Coire Odhar (pronounced *Corrie Ower*), 'dun-coloured corrie', which runs from behind the bothy on Devil's Point round to Cairn Toul. A stalker's path goes up the corrie from the bothy, a pleasant means of ascent to both hills, but it should be noted that it is a perilous corner in winter and should not be undertaken then except by experienced and adequately equipped mountaineers.

The bothy dates back to 1877 and was well used in the heyday of Victorian and Edwardian shooting. It later fell into disuse, but was still widely used as a haven or base for hill expeditions. The Cairngorm Club and other enthusiasts were responsible for its renovation in 1950 and for erecting the bridge.

7 *Clach nan Tailer*

This flat stone with ribbed lines tells an old tale of a wager that ended in disaster. The tailors made a bet one Hogmanay that they would dance at three 'dells' within twenty-four hours. 'Dell' is a corruption of the Gaelic word *dail*, a meadow or flat place, from which the place-name Dal comes. They successfully danced at Abernethy and Rothiemurchus and then set out through the Lairig for Dalmore, at the site of present-day Mar Lodge. The pass is a dangerous place in winter and they were overtaken by a blizzard and died while taking shelter in the lee of the stone that now bears their name.

8 *Garbh Coire*

This big corrie to the left (west) of the path is believed to be one of the most beautiful in the Cairngorms and is mentioned in one of the songs of the Cairngorms poet William Smith. It forms part of that great mountain, Braeriach (Am Braigh Riabhach, 'the brindled hill'), the second highest in the Cairngorms. It has another corrie leading off from it, Coire Bhrochain ('the corrie of gruel'), a name some think is somewhat fanciful and which is supposed to be derived from the fact of cattle at shieling times falling over the cliffs and being reduced to the consistency of porridge. Seton Gordon sent for analysis some bones found there and one was identified as the jawbone of an ox.

9 *The Pools of Dee*

Keep a look out for ptarmigan, mountain grouse, at the crest of the pass. They are frequently seen and nest there. At the summit of the pass the Allt na Criche, 'March burn', comes down from the plateau and disappears underground in the boulder fields, to reappear on the Dee side of the summit as one large and three smaller pools. Trout can be seen. The old name was Lochan Dubh na Lairige, 'the small black loch of the lairig'.

10 The Sinclair Memorial Hut

This building is Spartan in appearance and the path around it is very eroded. It commemorates Lieutenant-Colonel W. A. Sinclair, who died in these hills in 1954, and was opened in 1957. It arouses strong feelings among Cairngorms enthusiasts who feel that new buildings should not be erected.

11 Cairngorm Club footbridge

The Cairngorm Club is the oldest mountaineering club in Scotland. A group of Aberdeen hillwalkers decided to celebrate Queen Victoria's Golden Jubilee on 22 June 1887 by setting off rockets and fireworks on the summit of Ben Macdui. The six founder-members went to the Shelter Stone, on the shores of Loch Avon, spent the night there and the next day, on the shores of the loch, decided to form the Cairngorm Club for 'men and women of heroic spirit, and possessed of souls open to the influence and enjoyment of nature pure and simple as displayed among our loftiest mountains'. The club's formal constitution was drawn up in Aberdeen on 9 January 1889.

The Cairngorm Club footbridge

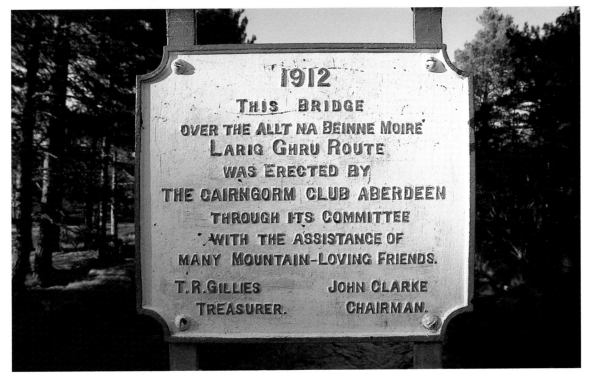

4.16

IN THE STEPS OF THE CLANS

STARTING POINT
The Meadows, in Callander, on the
A84 (57-628080)
FINISHING POINT
Ledcharrie Farm, Glen Dochart, on
the A85 (51-506281)
LENGTH
16 miles (26 km)
ASCENT
Highest points: 2884 ft (879 m) (Ben
Ledi) and 2685 ft (818 m) (Ben Vane).

SAFETY NOTE
Proper hill gear, including map and
compass, must be carried on this
walk.
ACCESS
It is usually necessary to arrange cars
at both ends, but a bus to and from
either end may be available on some
days (check locally).

This walk combines Highland mountains and passes which were much used in the days of the clans and which give magnificent views to many of the lochs and hills of the Southern Highlands. It is a strenuous walk, but has two escape routes for those who do not want to complete the entire journey. The traverse-walk includes rough terrain and some road-walking, as well as the ascent of Ben Ledi, one of the most attractive hills in the great front wall of the Grampians, which separate Lowland Scotland from the Highlands.

The second section of the walk, from Balquhidder (pronounced *Balwhidder*) of the Braes, crosses the historic Kirkton Pass and takes the walker to Glen Dochart and the A85 going north.

ROUTE DESCRIPTION (Maps 24–26)

At the west end of the town of Callander stands a prominent hotel, the Dreadnought, and just across the road is a car-park and grass flats beside the River Teith and known as the Meadows. At the west end of this parkland you pick up the start of a cycle track made out of the now-disused railway line. At the start, there is a prominent notice board with information about this former railway track, which leads to Balquhidder, and an old railway signal. The Meadows is sometimes prone to flooding and if it is not possible to walk across a lower path to the start of the cycle track, then proceed west along Callander main street until a gap in the streetside wall (L) takes you down to this track. Ahead lies the attractive bulk of Ben Ledi *(1)*, which dominates this section of the walk. Proceed along this cycle track and after a mile (1.6 km) you pass below the A82 which leads to nearby Kilmahog *(2)*.

Proceed straight on through the Pass of Leny (with attractive views of the River Leny on your R), one of the most strategically

*ALTERNATIVE STARTING POINT
Those who do not want to walk from Callander for the ascent of Ben Ledi can drive on the A84 to this car-park, which is attractively screened by trees.

*See ALTERNATIVE RETURN ROUTE overleaf.

View down Loch Voil from above Balquhidder

important passes in Scotland *(3)*, until you reach another car-park* and bridge at the start of Loch Lubnaig *(4)*. On the L (west) is a stile, and a somewhat eroded Forestry Commission path goes steeply up through the trees.

When you are clear of the trees there are some fine views up Loch Lubnaig and back to Callander and to some of the lower hills nearby. Cross a fence and a small burn (R) and proceed gradually uphill over occasionally boggy ground and due south, keeping the steep sides of the main part of the hill on your R (north). It is tempting to try and scramble straight up a prominent shale score or between the bluffs. Don't: the ground is more precarious than it looks.

Keep pushing gradually uphill on an intermittent track and southwards until you feel you can swing sharp R (west) and then north and easily gain the crest of the long, south ridge which runs down to Loch Venachar. Follow this undulating ridge over firm turf and some peaty sections to the summit, where there is an Ordnance Survey obelisk. The views to the south, to the bigger hills of the north, and to the lochs of the area can be stupendous *(5)*. Follow the northern ridge of Ben Ledi down to some broken ground above the Stank Glen (from the Gaelic, *stang*, pools).*

ALTERNATIVE RETURN ROUTE
(See previous page)

Walkers doing the circuit of Ben Ledi *only* can turn R (eastwards) down the Stank Glen, but the ground is steep and broken. A descent path is picked up below some prominent boulders and pinnacles which can be seen ahead, above and to the R as you descend, and the main path goes down through the trees on the south side of the Stank Glen burn. There is a deer fence below the boulders and pinnacles. Only very experienced hill trampers should descend from the summit down into Ben Ledi's northern corrie above the Stank Glen, as the ground is steep and boulder-strewn. There are safe lines, but they are sometimes hard for a newcomer to pick out. Once down at the foot of the Stank Glen, follow a forest track R (south), which leads into a broad track going southwards past cottages at Coireachrombie to the car-park at the Pass of Leny Bridge. This forest path which crosses a forest 'road' is sometimes difficult to pick up again at the far side of the forest 'road'.

*ALTERNATIVE FINISHING POINT
Those who do not want to proceed further over the Kirkton Pass can be picked up at the Balquhidder church, where there is some parking.

You reach a small loch, Lochan nan Corp ('the small loch of the dead') *(6)*. Then swing north-west to Stuc Dubh ('black peak'). The line of the route leads over undulating ground until one reaches the lower, eastern slope of Ben Vane, which is then followed to the summit. This hill also has outstanding views.

Follow the ridge down (northwards) to Glen Buckie and the farm at Ballimore where there is a metalled road. Proceed on this road. Go (L) at a junction just before you cross a bridge over the Balvaig River. This road takes you past the eastern end of Loch Voil to the Kirkton of Balquhidder where there are historic churches and the graves of the Highland hero Rob Roy MacGregor, his wife, and two sons *(7)*.

Immediately behind the nineteenth-century church* a path runs steeply uphill between the trees with a burn on your L. This is the Kirkton Glen and a few hundred yards (metres) up the path keep a lookout on your R for a Forestry Commission sign which says 'Creag an Tuirc' ('the crag of the boar'). It is well worth a short deviation on to a junction path, going R, which brings you out on top of this crag which gives magnificent views down the whole length of the Balquhidder Glen, over Loch Voil and Loch Doine and also back over Glen Buckie and some of the hills you have traversed *(8)*.

Return to the main path going up through the trees. You emerge on the open hillside and a small path takes you uphill. Ahead and right is a huge cliff, Creag an Eireannach ('the crag of the goat's leap') and some huge boulders. Pass beneath this crag and reach a small lochan at the head of the pass—another good place for a halt. Go through an old iron gate and proceed downhill. There are good views to the west (L) to two prominent mountains, Ben More and Stobinian, between the head of Balquhidder Glen and Crianlarich, and also to the Munro-tops of Creag Mhor ('big crag') and Sgiath Chuill ('the back wing') to the north of Glen Dochart.

Follow the east bank of the Ledcharrie burn (on your L as you descend) down to Ledcharrie Farm, passing below the old railway line. An intermittent track has occasional weathered waymarks. There is a car-parking space to the L (west) of the farm and you can arrange to be picked up there *(9)*. Some walkers walk the Kirkton Pass alone, Balquhidder to Ledcharrie, and then rest and walk back to Balquhidder.

1 Ben Ledi

The mountain dominates Callander. Its long south-east slope running down to Loch Venachar perhaps gave the mountain the name of Beinn an Leothaid ('the mountain of the gentle slope'), although Beinn le Dia ('the mountain of God') is

CONTINUE
ON MAP 25

MAP 24

STUC
DHUBH •662

ARDNANDAVE
HILL
•
715

LOCHAN
NAN CORP •⑥

BEN
LEDI △879
⑤

LOCH
LUBNAIG

A84

STANK GLEN

ALTERNATIVE ROUTE

④

ALTERNATIVE
STARTING POINT

SCALE 1:50 000

PASS OF LENY

③

LANDRANGER
Nº 57 AND Nº 51

Z

KILMAHOG
②

A821

A84

①

LOCH
VENACHAR

STARTING
POINT

CALLANDER

more likely. It is referred to familiarly by local people (as is Ben Nevis in Fort William) as 'the Ben'.

2   *Kilmahog*

The name is thought to derive from a combination of a corruption of the name of a shadowy Celtic saint called St Chug and *kil*, the Gaelic for a cell or ecclesiastical site. Another theory is that it derives from Cocca, a reputed robemaker and cook to St Patrick and St Columba. In past times Kilmahog housed a community of millers and James Hogg, the Ettrick shepherd, referred to Kilmahog in letters he sent to Sir Walter Scott during one of his jaunts through the Highlands and made a joke about the name being like his own. There is an ancient kirkyard nearby, which dates from the time of the Celtic Church.

3   *The Pass of Leny*

With its trees, brawling river and falls, this is a very beautiful place. The walking-route out to Ben Ledi follows the line through the pass of the old railway and also the route of the

Loch Lubnaig

A85   MAP 26

LEDCHARRIE

⑨

FINISHING POINT

DISMANTLED RAILWAY

LANDRANGER Nº 51 AND Nº 57

Ledcharrie Burn

N

CREAG AN EIREANNACH 791m

LOCH AN EIREANNACH

SCALE 1:50 000

KIRKTON GLEN

BRAES OF BALQUHIDDER

ALTERNATIVE FINISHING POINT

LOCH VOIL

⑦   ⑧

BALQUHIDDER

RIVER BALVAG

CONTINUED FROM MAP 25

eighteenth-century military road built by General Caulfeild, General Wade's subordinate, in a bid to control the unruly Jacobite clans. The A84 takes the other bank.

In Sir Walter Scott's epic poem 'The Lady of the Lake', which was published in 1810 and brought so many visitors to the area, he relates how the Fiery Cross, the mustering sign of the clans, was carried round the base of Ben Ledi and through this pass: 'Ben Ledi saw the cross of fire. It glanced like lightning up Strathire.' The name Leny derives from the Gaelic *lanaigh* ('boggy ground') and the pass is botanically very rich.

The famous Falls of Leny do not show their most boisterous face when you are walking on this track and are best viewed from the A84 side, but the strategic importance of the pass is clearly seen in its having two roads and a railway routed through it over the years.

4 *Loch Lubnaig*

This means 'the loch of the little bend'. The eastern shore in past times was held by the Clan Mackinlay, most of whom emigrated last century. Some migrated earlier to Northern Ireland and thence to the United States, where they eventually produced a president. The western shore was held by the Fergusons, and the prominent hill of Ardnandamh ('height of the stag') was one of their land titles.

5 *The summit of Ben Ledi*

The mountain's summit is connected with La Buidhe Bealltuinn, 'the yellow day of the fires of Bel'. In past times, on the first day of May, the old Celtic new year, young folk from the parishes of Callander, Buchanan, Balquhidder and Aberfoyle met there to commemorate an old Druidic rite, the lighting of the Bealltuinn (Beltane) fires. Bel (from Be'uill, 'life of all') had been the early Celtic sun god. Hearth fires were extinguished before midnight to symbolize the dying of the old year. New sacrificial fires were lit on hills and the hearth fires relit from these flames. Sometimes cattle were driven between fires on the lower ground. A fire was lit on the summit and a special cake, a bannock, was made and cut into slices and shared out. Whoever drew a marked portion had to skip through the embers. The practice had died out by the nineteenth century. Votive offerings were also made to birds and animals allegedly harmful to crops or beasts: the wolf, fox, eagle, raven and hooded crow.

6 *Lochan nan Corp*

A strong local tradition has it that a funeral party walking from Gleann Casaig on the north-west side of Ben Ledi to St Bride's chapel on Loch Lubnaig-side tried to cross this small

loch when it was frozen. The ice broke and many drowned. There is no factual evidence other than that the route was a well-known funeral or coffin route and the name may simply derive from that, a known spot on a well-used hill-crossing.

7 *Balquhidder*

The name means 'the township in the back country'. The lands here were in Crown ownership as far back as the time of James IV and formed part of the dowry given to the Welsh princess, Margaret Tudor. It was a glen of the Clans MacGregor, Ferguson, Stewart and MacLaren. The MacGregors and MacLarens fought in 1532 over the right to be seated first in church. In the old kirkyard are the graves of Rob Roy MacGregor, famed cattle dealer and warrior, his wife Mary (Helen) and their sons Coll and Robert.

The ruined church nearby dates from 1631 and is itself on top of a pre-Reformation church dating back to the thirteenth century. A monastic cell, the Oratory of St Angus, the patron saint of Balquhidder, stood in a field below the church. The Rev. Robert Kirk, Gaelic scholar, student of faery lore and author of *The Secret Commonwealth of Elves, Fauns and Fairies*, ministered here from 1664 to 1685. The present church of 1855 is worth a visit.

Sir Walter Scott and Robert Louis Stevenson both brought Balquhidder into their writings and William Wordsworth wrote a poem about the local girls singing Gaelic songs as they worked in the fields now covered by conifer forests.

8 *Creag an Tuirc*

This was the rallying or gathering place of Clan MacLaren in past times. The modern clan society has erected a cairn on top. There are superb views over the Kirkton of Balquhidder, to Glen Buckie and down the length of Balquhidder Glen and over Loch Voil and Loch Doine to Inverlochlarig, where Rob Roy died. The opening shots of the film *Geordie*, the story of a small boy who grew up to be an Olympic hammer-thrower, were filmed from this crag. The Kirkton Pass itself is a right-of-way and an ancient hill-crossing route. It was used by cattle drovers in the last century and earlier, when thousands of cattle were driven from the Highlands to be sold at the great fairs in the south.

9 *Glen Dochart*

The glen links with Strath Fillan to form one of Scotland's great east-west passes. Its name derives from a Gaelic word meaning 'scouring': the river Dochart is often fast-flowing. The Clan MacNab once held sway here but were absorbed in the sixteenth and seventeenth centuries by the expansionist policies of the Breadalbane Campbells.

Previous page: Ben Ledi from Callander

120

SELECTED WALKS IN THE NORTH-WEST HIGHLANDS AND ISLANDS

Hamish Brown

Highland Cattle

INTRODUCTION

The Great Glen, Glen Alba, that great geographical tear-fault with Loch Ness and the Caledonian Canal filling it (from Fort William to Inverness) is a psychological as well as a physical landmark. Improved roads and more reliable cars have made it much easier to reach, yet somehow, even to walkers living in the Scottish Lowlands, never mind south of the border, there is an aura of remoteness, toughness and other-worldliness about the lands 'beyond the Great Glen'. Hopefully, the eight, very varied, walks described here will lure the curious traveller into that magical region.

Magical it is, as if the Creator, having worked up through the land, suddenly began to be more lavish in his use of the spectacular. The Outer Hebrides of course believe they are God's jewels, scattered before He sat back on the Seventh Day. The beauty has a diamond hardness about it. This is Kipling's 'edge of cultivation'. Man hangs on with a limpet's tenacity here, where there are some of the oldest rocks in the world. Glaciers have cut deep into the mountains, and the vegetation is as thin as a scarecrow's coat. Sea and sky are like living beasts, pawing and knawing at the land. Beyond the Great Glen the landscape goes into overdrive and, for the walker new to it, the experience can be a bit breathless.

To select just eight walks from this wealth is like asking a botanist to pick eight flowers from the flora of the British Isles. A score of islands and a hundred bens and glens spring to mind. Skye, being the Valhalla of the Scottish mountains, chose itself. Everyone, some day, has to discover the Cuillin. Ben More in Mull offers the only other island 'Munro' and is a favourite of many. We must apologize to Shetland, Orkney, the whole Outer Hebrides and a dozen Inner Hebridean islands. Maybe it is as well: islands can be addictive.

Coastal walking in Scotland has hardly been discovered yet so I felt one walk of that type was needed. The Stacks of Duncansby are unforgettable, even if one of the easiest walks in this book. The Glenelg Glens circuit brings in the richness of prehistory, which is so much a part of the north and west and shows a good day can be followed without having to climb any summit. But summits are a lure. Torr Beag on that walk is a small hill with a big view.

Beinn a' Bha'ach Ard I include slightly tongue-in-cheek. It is not often climbed, not being a Munro. It is a Corbett however and illustrates the wealth of attractive walking, and superlative summit views, to be had from hills near, yet below, the Plimsoll line of 3000 ft (914 m). Be warned though: Corbetts can also be habit-forming.

The next three routes all offer the option of reaching Munro height within the framework of longer traverses or circuits. Kintail/Affric, Mull and Torridon are notable tourist showplaces but we go behind the scenes. Legs, not wheels, lead to the real performances. And we can write our own script! These can be serious undertakings. 'Take care, or the undertaker does the taking,' as one of my mentors cheerfully put it.

In the north-west the extraordinary peaks seem to straggle across the watery world like a herd of petrified mammoths. There had to be something from Assynt and Quinag, a mountain of mountains, is as fine as any. And then there is Skye. Poucher called his book on the island *The Magic of Skye.* Magic it is: Aslan country, not a tame country at all. I trust you are roaring to go!

Loch Torridon

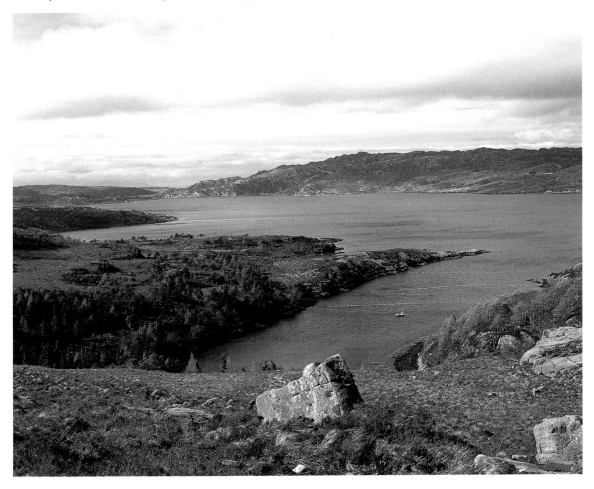

THE STACKS OF DUNCANSBY

STARTING AND FINISHING
POINT
John o' Groats at the end of the A9 in
Caithness (12-380734). The
Ordnance Survey 1:25,000 Pathfinder
map ND37/47 gives more names of
interest and is useful for showing
fences and other details.
LENGTH
6 miles (9 km)
ASCENT
330 ft (100 m)

ACCESS

John o' Groats lies at the northern
end of the A9 in Caithness and this is
a walk for early summer, before the
honeypot buzzes with swarms of
trippers. The road-end has little to
recommend it and is not even the
most northerly or north-easterly
corner of Britain. However, there are
useful things like toilets, a camp site,
bed-and-breakfast places, a nearby
youth hostel, and some public
transport, including a passenger ferry
across the Pentland Firth to Orkney.
There are also some genuinely interesting tourist attractions: a pottery
and a colourful candle factory,
industries of vital importance in such
a remote rural area.

This walk is both short and easy. In this case, though, small is
not only beautiful but also spectacular. Were the Stacks of
Duncansby sited other than in the extreme north-east corner of
Scotland, they would be very well known. John o' Groats,
undeniably a tourist attraction, lies only 2 miles (3 km) away as
the crow flies, but 90% of tourists never go more than ¼ mile
(400 m) from their cars. The Stacks are all ours, serendipity for
the walker.

ROUTE DESCRIPTION (Map 27)

From the harbour (1) walk eastwards for ⅝ mile (1 km)
between fields and sea with the tidal sands held in place, as it
were, by the nails of seaward rocks. Just before Robert's Haven
and the bulge of the Ness of Duncansby is the site of an early
chapel. Between the Ness (Norse for 'headland') and the Island
of Stroma, the sea is often in turmoil: this is the tide-race of the
Boars of Duncansby (2). The Bay of Sannick is another sandy
shelter, where waders may gather (3). Leave the bay where the
burn flows into it, for the character of the walk changes. From
now on it is cliff-top walking rather than seaside strolling. The
cliff edge is fenced off until nearly opposite the Stacks of
Duncansby. For me, Duncansby Head (4), thrusting out into the
sea, is the geographical counterpart of Land's End.

Working down southwards, detour round the Geo of
Sclaites. From the point of its south side Humlies Hole is a pillar
only just connected to the cliff—a stack for the future. There is
a cave in the back of the rift and an off-shore stack called The
Knee and another, under the cliff, Gibb's Crag.

As you move on, the twin Stacks of Duncansby seem to
dodge in and out from the red sandstone cliffs. There are two of
these fangs (and the stumps of other molars long ago worn-
down to the gums of the sea), rufous and green, vertical rock,

The sands at John o' Groats

vertical vegetation, every horizontal seemingly possessed by birds, from attic fulmars to basement shags. Another prow of cliff is being chiselled off by nature and the Stacks have holes through them. Nothing is still, not even the rock itself *(5)*. The cliffs reach a maximum of 265 ft (81 m) on Hill of Crogodale, ⅓ mile (500 m) south of the Stacks, a good turning point for the walk.

Return by the same route to the hollow below the lighthouse hill, then cut across to pick up the lighthouse road and walk along it into the scattered crofts and houses of John o' Groats. Alternatively aim directly towards the houses, picking up a track off the moors leading into the 'school' shown on maps (i.e. head due north-west from Hill of Crogodale).

1 The Story of John o' Groats

Jan de Groot is buried at Canisbay Church, 2½ miles (4 km) west of John o' Groats. This old Danish (Viking)-influenced church is near the Castle of Mey, the home of the Queen Mother, who attends services when in the north. The John o' Groats name has a popular derivation but an explanation did not appear in print until the 1791 *Statistical Account*. This tells of three de Groot brothers (of Dutch origins) settling in the area in the fifteenth century. At an annual family gathering a great quarrel arose over precedence and Jan (John) solved this issue by building an octagonal house with eight doors and an octagonal table in the centre so that each son could enter on level terms. The house had gone by the time eighteenth-century travellers arrived but the hotel has re-created this

127

architectural oddity. The most northerly point is Dunnet Head, 11 miles (18 km) west of here, another spectacular 400-ft (120 m) cliff bluff with a lighthouse on top. Timothy Pont, the great cartographer, was minister of Dunnet Kirk.

2 *Duncansby*

This name is older than that of John o' Groats. Duncan (Dungal) was a Celtic *mormaor* (earl) whose name the Norse gave to the district. The first Atlantic chart (1569) has it as Dungesbi. The Head was named on Ptolemy's map, the first-ever (first century AD) map to show Britain.

3 *Bird-life*

Turnstones, purple sandpipers, ringed plovers, and dunlins (red-backed sandpipers) are the commonest shore visitors in winter. Rarer are bar-tailed godwits, knots and sanderlings. Corncrakes are rare now and birds like the snow bunting and redwing are at the southern edge of their northern range. Puffins, guillemots, razorbills, kittiwakes, shags and *tysties* (black guillemots) are some of the cliff nesters, along with pipits and rock doves. Gannets and both great and Arctic skuas can be watched offshore.

On the northern sands you may also find 'groaty buckies', small, pink-tinted cowries, and the only cowrie found in European waters. Seals are common and the area has several stories connected with seals, the *selkies* of the sea, who could take on human form. Eric Linklater's *Sealskin Trousers* is a famous modern story on this old theme.

4 *Duncansby Head*

When I walked from John o' Groats to Land's End, a story told in *Hamish's Groat's End Walk* (Gollancz/Paladin), I began at Duncansby Head, with the Stacks of Duncansby being almost symbols of the journey. Most walkers, rather than Groat's End racers, have expressed the same feelings: Duncansby Head is the worthier starting or finishing point.

5 *The Stacks*

'No traveller, when he comes to John o' Groats, will repent a visit to the Head. The Stalks [*sic*] of Duncansby are two pyramidal pillars of natural freestone-rock. They rear their fantastic summits a great way into the air and strike the eye as the huge spires of some old, magnificent Gothic pile.' So was the scene described in the 1791 *Statistical Account*. The stacks are locally Muckle (big) Stack and Peedie (small) Stack and there is a much smaller third stack. They are made of old red sandstone, the horizontal strata of which give the stepped-pyramid effect. Sea eagles once nested on their crests.

Previous page: *The Stacks of Duncansby*

2.18

Beinn a' Bha'ach Ard

STARTING AND FINISHING
POINT
Car-park on the Glen Strathfarrar
road by Culligran power station.
(26-378404), but see note below
about access to the glen.

Use the second series 1:50,000
map for accuracy.
LENGTH
7½ miles (12 km)
ASCENT
2900 ft (880 m).

This hill, whose name is pronounced *Ben ah Vaichart,* is a classic example of the good things to be found in the Scottish Highlands without subjecting yourself to the historical tyranny of Munro altitude (3000 ft/914 m). The lower parts are covered in attractive native birch forest and above lie easy heather or grassy slopes leading to a notable view-point, not only of the mountains but of the lowland country round the Moray Firth. This is a walk for a clear day in early summer.

Route Description (Map 28)

The entrance to the Culligran power station *(1)* is rather hidden in the trees, but the unsurfaced road that passes it is clear enough. Please do not park on the power-station side of the road; there is plenty of space opposite or near by.

Rocks in Glen Strathfarrar

ACCESS

The road from Struy up Glen Strathfarrar is not open freely to vehicular
traffic, there being a locked gate at
Inchmore (26-396405), but permis-
sion/admission can normally be obtained from the house beside the gate.
(Check beforehand by telephoning
Struy (046376)260.) Much of the
lower glen is nature reserve and the
upper parts are deer forest. The limit
on the number of cars makes the
wildlife much more noticeable and
also allows you to relish the superb
peace and quiet. After climbing the
hill you can round off the day with a
drive up to Loch Monar and back.
There is nothing to prevent anyone
walking up the glen at any time (cars
can be parked, off-road, just before
the gate) but the hill should not be
ascended from mid-August to the
third week in October, as this is the
deer-stalking season. At that time
disturbance can spoil the necessary
cull (a vital part of the local economy)
and there is a risk from high-velocity
rifle fire.

The road is used by the estate (2) as well as providing access
for the hydro-electric service. It rises steeply then swings L to
wander through some fine birch woods (3). A track bearing off
back half-R leads to the top station of the power station's
pipeline and shortly after there is another R branch (shown as a
footpath on the 1:50,000 map). Ignore these for the main road
westwards. Roe-deer can sometimes be seen and in season there
are areas of lush blaeberries (bilberries) to excite the taste buds
and stain fingers and tongue.

The wood opens out as the road follows the glen of the Neaty
Burn. A power line runs parallel with the road and river, a river
which never flows very full as, ⅝ mile (1 km) along, you find a
small water-intake dam. The water is borrowed for creating
power (4). The rough road ends at this point.

There is no path shown on the map but one runs up the east
bank of the Neaty Burn from here. It is not a 'made' path but is
the result of 'go-anywhere' vehicles carrying down deer from
the hill. In less than ⅓ mile (500 m) it reaches the path shown
on the map and takes over from what was once a superb
stalkers' path from the days when ponies brought down the
deer. The old stalkers' path below this level is now completely
overgrown and quite impossible to see in places.

Continue up the track on the east bank to the junction with
the stream descending directly from Beinn a' Bha'ach Ard, a
somewhat damper area, and then closely follow the line of this
side stream, the Allt Doire Bhuig ('stream of the damp wood'),
on good firm ground. (The track goes on up the glen for another
⅝ mile (1 km) and then swings off uphill to the west.) In June
the line of the Allt Doire Bhuig shows a succession of beautiful,
and often rare, mountain flowers (5).

The stream is welcome on a hot day, so have a good drink
before it peters out. When there is no burn to follow, just head
straight up the steep slope northwards to gain the easy west
ridge of the hill. This leads gently along to the final cone of the
summit bump, where there is an Ordnance Survey obelisk and
cairn and a view with a dramatic sweep to the east (6).

Real alternative routes off the hill are not practical, but the
west ridge could be followed to the Neaty Burn or the ups and
downs of the craggier south ridge could be followed as long as
the heather remains close cropped and easy to walk on. Head
down to the Neaty Burn when the going becomes rougher but
be careful in working through the minor crags.

The return by the Neaty Burn and the hydro road is no dull
repetition but rewards the walker with changing views and
wildlife. Few good summits can be scaled so easily or give such a
sample of the true variety of Highland scenery. Though not a

Munro, this hill, small by Scottish standards, is still higher than most in England. The summit view emphasizes that.

1 Culligran Power Station
 The power station is actually hidden underground. All we see is the entrance. It is fed by a tunnel from the dammed Loch Beannacharan further up the glen and also by an aqueduct from above Culligran farm which captures all the drainage

MAP 28

BEINN A' △
BHA'ACH ARD ⑥

ALLT DOIRE BHUIG

⑤

NEATY BURN

ALTERNATIVE DECENT

PATHFINDER
SHEET NH 24/34

SCALE 1:25000

N

④

PATH NOT ADVISED

POWER
LINE

STARTING AND
FINISHING POINT

③

②

①

CULLIGRAN
FALLS

CULLIGRAN
POWER
STATION

RIVER FARRAR

Near Culligran

east of our hill. The Neaty Burn is also tapped. As this is an important salmon river, there is a fish lift at Loch Beannacharan and the Culligran falls have also been made easier for fish to pass. The falls lie ⅓ mile (500 m) up from here and are worth seeing. The rock strata are much folded.

2 *Highland estates*

Red deer were originally forest animals. Being forced by our man-altered landscape to live on the hostile heights, their numbers have to be strictly controlled. Even so, a bad winter or spring can see many die of starvation, a fact overlooked by the sentimental objectors to shooting deer. Remote estates are often the only source of local employment. They have built the paths which we, as walkers, find so useful for our pleasurable pastime.

3 *Birch woods*

Birch woods like this go back to the last Ice Age. Birch is one of the first colonizers of waste ground, river flushes, etc. The trees were often coppiced in olden times. Bundles of birch were laid on the bogs of Rannoch Moor as a base for the railway line.

4 *Borrowed water*

This is an apt description. Loch Monar at the head of Glen Strathfarrar has a huge catchment area, including aqueducts capturing streams well down below the level of its two dams. The water is piped to a power station by Loch Beannacharan and that loch's waters are piped to the Culligran power station (taking in the Neaty Burn *en passant*). The Farrar waters join the much-used Affric-River Glass waters and, on what becomes the River Beauly, there are two dams at Aigas and Kilmorack before the water is returned to flow into the sea. At Aigas one can see the fish lift in operation in the summer months.

5 *Mountain flowers*

I noted cow wheat, cloudberry, tormentil, chickweed-wintergreen, dwarf cornel, lousewort, slender St John's wort, besides ling, both heathers, cotton grass and various attractive mosses.

6 *The summit view*

The Black Isle is really a peninsula between the Beauly Firth and the Cromarty Firth. It dominates the view seaward. There is attractive country between here and Inverness and a glimpse of the distant Cairngorms. To the west and south are a seemingly endless array of mountains, the Lapaichs and Affric hills being the highest hills north of the Great Glen.

3.19

THE GLENELG GLENS CIRCUIT

STARTING AND FINISHING
POINT
The Glenelg Inn, in Glenelg
(33-814193.)
LENGTH
14 miles (22 km)
ASCENT
820 ft (250 m)

ACCESS
Glenelg is so hemmed in by hills that
all early access tended to be by sea,
and there is still a summer vehicle
ferry across to Kylerhea on Skye. As
part of the taming of the Highlands
the military built a road from Glen
Shiel over Mam Ratagan in the
eighteenth century, and this remains
the only landward access to the
village. A post bus runs from Kyle of
Lochalsh (railway terminal) to
Glenelg and Arnisdale, otherwise one
drives or walks! The road is clearly
signposted from Shiel Bridge on the
A87 and gives one of the most
spectacular hill drives in Scotland,
with a famous view to Loch Duich
and the Five Sisters of Kintail.

Glenelg is a hamlet on the west coast which has had its ups and
downs in the struggle to survive in such a remote, well-
defended corner of wild country. That very wilderness makes
the area particularly attractive to the walker and while this is
technically an easy circuit (most of it on roads) there is still a
grand feel of raw nature and man's old struggle to survive.

Oh let them be left, wildness and wet;

Long live the weeds and the wilderness yet.

(Hopkins, 'Inversnaid')

ROUTE DESCRIPTION (Map 29)

The Glenelg Inn is a good starting-point *(1)* and will no doubt
be even more appreciated on becoming the terminal point. The
village has a short street with one shop cum post office,
telephone box, primary school and forestry houses off the
straight avenue leading towards Glen More. Just past the
telephone box a short diversion should be taken along a track to
see the Bernera Barracks *(2)*, the termination of the original
military road.

The long, straight avenue out of the village leads to a junction
by The Smiddy. Here is the old school and the local cemetery.
The road L terminates in 2 miles (3 km) at the slipway for the
Kylerhea vehicle ferry to Skye.

After 2¾ miles (4.5 km) turn off at a fork R signposted for
Moyle just before the Mam Ratagan road begins to climb steeply
up above the glen. You will be able to look to it from several
places in the next hour or two. The summit of this pass is 1112
ft (339 m) *(3)*.

As you look up the glen, there is a knobbly dome of hill
ahead, Sgurr Mhic Bharraich, which the more energetic could
take in *(4)*. The hill is a Corbett and a notable view-point. The
more conical hill is simply the last top on the long northern arm

of ridge leading from the Saddle, one of the grandest mountains in Scotland, normally climbed from Glen Shiel. At Scallasaig there is a telephone box beside the shepherd's house and a bridge across to Braeside. The path up the L bank to Suardalin should be avoided: the path is not always clear and the going is 'moist'. Continue along the metalled road, which enters the forest at a cattle grid and becomes a dirt road at the bend above Moyle.

Much of Ratagan forest has been felled through the 1980s, and replanted. A row of deciduous trees along the track's edge will make a pleasant avenue for future generations. In the rushy field to the R there are several ruins, the long-dead clachan of Lionachan. When the forestry road forks, bear R. After ⅝ mile (1 km) there is another fork and you bear R again, through a gate and across the bridge over the Glenmore River. Those heading for Sgurr Mhic Bharraich can take the L fork.

The road curves up to enter the large upper Glen More plantations. Just before reaching the forest break off R

Glen More from the Mam Ratagan road

Right: *Bernera Barracks.*

Opposite: *Detail of a broch*

(untracked) to follow the gently-angled ridge up to the top of Torr Beag. The summit is a prehistoric *dun* and the view through to Beinn Sgritheall (Sgriol) is of classic beauty *(5)*. Torr Beag is the perfect spot for a picnic, on a sunny day.

There is a clear view across to Mam Ratagan, with cars reduced to the size of toys, and in the hollow below the hill stands the lonely ex-shepherd's house of Suardalin (pronounced *Swordland*). The big walled field and the sheep-fank are still in use. The house is a bothy *(6)* and on a wet day can be used for an indoor picnic. It is as well to head down east a bit and circle round to reach the estate road which descends under its western slopes. Follow the road on down to Strath a'Chomair.

When the road and river turn sharply north and drop steeply, the fort of Dun Grugaig on the lip of the gorge can be seen over on the L. Go across to inspect the site. It is like half a broch (of which more below) but half was all that it was necessary to build as the gorge wall is a natural defence for the rest.

Walk on down the glen road but at the first passing place on the R after Balvraid note the chambered cairn just over the fence. The passage and chamber can still be made out and a big capping stone is precariously propped up. A bit further on, the road crosses a bridge and passes tight between river and steep hillside. As soon as it opens out again go through the gate, L about 50 yards (45 m) out in the middle of this open space there is a cairn on which sits a fine cup-marked stone *(7)*.

After ⅝ mile (1km), speculations on cup-markings will give way to wonder as the brochs come in sight: Dun Troddan and Dun Telve, which (after Mousa on a Shetland island) are the

137

best-preserved examples of a unique Scottish architectural feature *(8)*.

After another ⅝ mile (1 km) of pleasant valley, a gate on the L gives a view across to one of Scotland's most attractive waterfalls, the Eas Mor Cuil an Duin *(9)*. There are further falls above the big one (invisible from the valley) and the next stream west also descends in a series of cascades; the wild mountain flanks a strange contrast to the fertile valley bottom. At the last big bend the river is biting into a huge alluvial gravel deposit. Walk by the alder-held burn down to the Arnisdale road at Eilanreach, the local 'big house'. Glenelg is indicated at 1¼ miles (2 km) distant.

1   *Glenelg Inn*

This was, till some years ago, more interestingly called the Telford Inn, after the famous engineer who updated the road over Mam Ratagan. Shiel Bridge's bridge is one of his sturdy structures still in regular use.

2   *Bernera Barracks*

Built in 1722, this is now a roofless ruin but with the walls still largely intact, so the plan is easy to see. Those who know the Ruthven Barracks by the A9 at Kingussie will have a decided feeling of *déjà vu*.

3   *Mam Ratagan*

Early descriptions of crossing this pass occur in the journals of Samuel Johnson and James Boswell. On their 1773 journey the hefty doctor had to employ two ponies alternately.

4   *Sgurr Mhic Bharraich*

This Corbett (2552 ft, 778 m) has steep slopes with quite a bit of crag, and the forestry plantings rule out any approach from the Mam Ratagan. An old footpath from Shiel Bridge to Glen More, however, runs over the pass to the south of it and gives a reasonable ascent, from either end. Keep on the north side of the Glenmore River to the end of the forest road and head upstream and across to the ruin of Bealachasan. The footpath is not always clear, but it becomes more so up to the pass with its lochan, from where the summit can be tackled. Return the same way. This diversion adds about 2½ hours to the walk.

5   *Torr Beag*

This *dun* or fort is largely a naturally defended situation, being well ringed with crags, but across the one easy place of access (our line of approach) the defenders erected a wall. The tumbled remains of this can still be seen.

6   *Suardalin*

A bothy is an open refuge, often with little or no furnishings, but a welcome haven to walkers in midge and monsoon

seasons. The Mountain Bothies Association (MBA) maintains scores of such buildings. Information from New Members Secretary, 26 Rycroft Avenue, Deeping St James, Peterborough, England. This particular bothy is looked after by the Braes o Fife Mountaineering Club (BFMC) from Fife, who have spent many days pointing, roofing and dealing with woodworm and also with vandalism. Though there are acres of woodland nearby, people still burn the shepherd's sheep-fank gate or saw out roof timbers.

7 *Cup-marked stones*
The origins and meanings of these pock-markings are a complete mystery. They are found throughout the British Isles but whole areas have none while other have dozens of sites. Sometimes the cup-marks are circled by rings and other patterns. As you walk on you can produced your own speculations! Shire Archaeology 47, 'Rock Carvings of North Britain', by S. Beckensall, is a recommended booklet.

8 *Brochs*
The experts date brochs to the Iron Age period (100 BC–AD 200). Norse raiders were centuries later. The Romans (contemporaries of the indigenous population certainly) never made any moves to justify such defences. Why were they built? Their sudden appearance is also startling. It is as if some whizz-kid sat down at his drawing board to design the very latest technological defensive system—and came up with the broch.

Note the small entrance, defended by a side chamber, a pattern repeated in the entrance to the mural staircase. The notice at Dun Troddan points out the discovery of post holes which, with the roof-height ring of stones, indicate structures built inside. At Dun Telve there is a second of these scarcements near the top. Was the whole roofed over in fact? Before leaving Dun Troddan, walk round the back to gain the exterior impression. Dun Telve's entrance has a blockhouse outside it, a rare extra defence for brochs. If brochs appeal, Caisteal Grugaig (33-867251), is worth a visit while in the area. Its stonework is of cyclopean proportions; the triangular lintel alone must weigh more than a ton (1000 kg). Shire Archaeology 53, 'Brochs of Scotland' by J. N. G. Ritchie, is a good booklet on the subject.

9 *Eas Mor Cuil an Duin*
Eas Mor means 'big fall'. Cuil an Duin is 'nook of the fort', perhaps after Castle Chalamine, a *dun* at 815174. Nothing is visible now but a scramble up is rewarded by a view of falls, brochs and the Sound of Sleat: a strategic site.

Previous page: *Glenelg Bay and the Sound of Sleat*

3.20

THE GATES OF AFFRIC

STARTING AND FINISHING
POINT
Car-park on minor road to
Dorusduain, Strath Croe, Kintail, off
A87 (33-977223).
LENGTH
10 miles (16 km)
ASCENT
2625 ft (800 m)

This is a circular walk which incorporates two big hill passes. Several hills could be added to the route and there are even alternative circuits, the area being a great jumble of hills and glens, so typical of the west of Scotland. This is certainly not tame country and the straightforward walk is quite as demanding as, say, an ascent of Snowdon or Scafell. An ascent is perhaps welcomed as a chance to expand the view, the circuit itself being hemmed in by some big, famous peaks. Apart from the challenging nature of this walk, it is perhaps bigness that is the abiding memory of the day.

ACCESS

The start lies up a side glen off the A87 'Road to the Isles' as it sweeps round the head of Loch Duich in Kintail. The paths are old rights-of-way and Gleann Gaorsaic is National Trust for Scotland land so there is no access problem. Ben Attow is also owned by the Trust, but deer-stalking may take place on other hills.

The A87 is left just north of the causeway turning R onto a minor road with a signpost indicating that Morvich is 1 mile (1.6 km) and Innis a' Chro 2 miles (3 km) distant. After ⅛ mile (1 km) fork L (33-955215) onto an even smaller road, with no signpost. This runs along Strath Croe, passing the smart house of Lienassie, progress slowed by a series of artificial humps on the road, passes a sheep-fank, and enters Forestry Commission land. At 977223 there is a small car-park beside a road with a signpost indicating that Glomach Falls is 4 miles (6.5 km) away. This is all rather obscured by writing on the 1:50 000 map. Do not try to drive on to Dorusduain. The metalled section ends just beyond the car-park and the track beyond is hardly fit for cars. Park in the car-park.

Previous page: *Deer in the Dorusduain forest*

ROUTE DESCRIPTION (Maps 30, 31)

From the car-park walk along the rough track to Dorusduain (the sign reading 'Private road to Dorusduain only' does not apply to pedestrians). The road is gated but a side gate allows walkers through. Half-way from the gate to the sadly derelict house, turn R down by four larch trees to another walkers' gate in the fence above the river. The path drops down to a footbridge and climbs out of the gorge on the other side, landing you on a very wet level of hillside. The path from Morvich and Innis a' Chro along the south side of Strath Croe lies 325 ft (100 m) over, contouring the foot of the steeper, drier hillside. Splash over to join it *(1)*.

The path leads on to swing round and up Gleann Choinneachain, above a considerable gorge that moats the hill of A'Ghlas-bheinn across the way *(2)*. The path climbs steadily and after the stream draining the southern corries is crossed, it climbs across and then zig-zags. At the top of the zig-zags a cairn shows a stalkers' path breaking off R. This leads up the corrie, to end on the neck of the Meall a' Bhealaich ridge, which gives easy access to the edge of the huge plateau of Ben Attow. This big hill is a quite reasonable addition to the route. It is a massive sprawl of hill with an equally big view *(3)*. A walk even part of the way up the corrie is recommended for the slabby cliffs of the double corrie are unusual. Deer are often seen, too.

The Bealach an Sgairne ('the pass of rumbling') is a narrow defile, deep-set and lonely, and is sometimes referred to as the Gates of Affric. There is indeed a portal-like quality of a door suddenly opening to look down into upper Glen Affric (Gleann Gniomhaidh).

There is quite a feeling of commitment in passing through the Gates and down the far side. The country is utterly devoid of human landmarks. Glen Gniomhaidh sounds like a name out of Narnia, as does Gleann Gaorsaic. Once you can see down both glens clearly, stop and have a good look, for *you* are going to have to make some decisions. Pick a route round Loch a' Bhealaich that will take you into Gleann Gaorsaic. This loch does not drain east through Glen Affric. A gentle watershed holds it back and it flows off to the north.

Gleann Gaorsaic is a mess of peat bogs and no real route is recommended. It is Hobson's choice as to which side of the loch is taken: for 2¾ miles (4.5 km) there is almost no loss of height and you wend past lochans and peat bogs. It is a good area for spotting deer *(4)*. Somewhere before the glen curves to the west and begins to steepen, make sure that you are on the L (west) bank. The gentle angle changes somewhat.

The Falls of Glomach are generally regarded as the second highest in Britain, but they have one of the longest uninterrupted drops of water. They are frustrating falls, for the water plunges down into such a perpendicularly-cut gorge that only the top of the falls is readily visible. More adventurous exploration is not recommended. There have been a number of accidents in which people slipped on the steep slopes edging the gorge. With care you can take a zig-zag track down to a platform which gives the best view of the falls. The initial plunge is of 80 ft (24 m) and it then breaks into two falls which curtain down into invisible depths, 350 ft (110 m) below.

A good path ascends from lonely Glen Elchaig and heads back over the Bealach na Sroine to Strath Croe. This is an old 'coffin road' *(5)*. Simply follow the path steeply to start and then across gentler ground. A' Ghlas-bheinn thrusts up its craggy features to the south and once over the watershed the path angles steadily down into a deep-set glen, Glen Leiod Ghaineamhaich, one of three major feeders which meet at the head of Glen Croe. Across the way, the western burn, especially after rain, falls down in a long mare's tail fall, the Eas Ban ('white fall').

Cross a footbridge just above the confluence of the northern feeder *(6)* and pull up onto a turning place at the end of a forestry road. A certain amount of care is advisable: the route is well signposted for walkers heading up (but not down) the glen and a wrong fork can lead you well astray in the forest. Take the R fork on leaving the road-end. This angles down to cross the river, pulls up and merges with another road before continuing round and down. At the next split keep along R, where there is a gate, traversing above Dorusduain. The road becomes roughly surfaced as it snakes down to the car-park.

Opposite: *Rushing waters in Glen Leoid Ghaineamhaich*

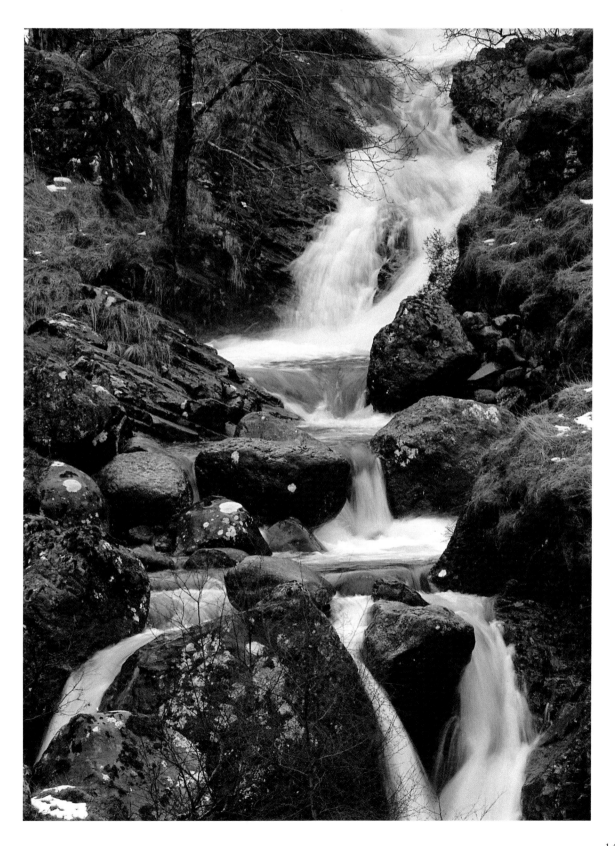

1 *Morvich*

There is a small camp-site here and in the summer the National Trust of Scotland has its Kintail Countryside Centre with information and displays. The motor road ends before Innis a' Chro (Chrotha) and a stalkers' path continues up the glen, which you join.

2 *A' Ghlas-bheinn*

This is a modest Munro in altitude (3010 ft, 918 m) but it is no easy hill, with huge cliff-edged gulleys coming down and the base defended by forest and river. Access from our passes is no easy option for both ridges, south and north, are an endless succession of craggy bumps. The east face is not attractive. Probably the easiest ascent is from the Bealach na Sroine, skirting the worst of the craggy bumps, and returning the same way.

3 *Ben Attow (Beinn Fhada)*

This big hill (3385 ft, 1032 m) has a large plateau, much edged by the cliffs of surrounding corries, so its ascent is best kept for a clear day unless you are willing to be tested on navigation skills. There is a perfectly good path up to the plateau rim. I do not know why the Ordnance Survey are keeping it a secret. By using the path up you can gain a fine view-point, not only over the giants of Affric and the Five Sisters, but out to Skye and the islands.

4 *Red deer*

On Loch a' Bhealaich there is an islet which is well-wooded because it is out of reach of deer, as are many of the gorges seen today. All the hillsides were once similarly wooded but the deer, driven artificially by man to live on the heights, will graze any accessible growth. There is no regeneration and so much of Scotland's hill ground remains a wet desert.

5 *Coffin roads*

As the name suggests, these were routes over which funeral processions were wont to travel. Clansmen greatly desired to be buried in their own country and on a graveyard such as St Duthac's (L. Duich) several routes were likely to converge.

6 *Stalkers' paths*

Another path uses this stream, and the pass beyond, to reach Glen Elchaig. People are often puzzled by paths in the mountains which seemingly (as several near here) stop in the middle of nowhere. These are basically old 'made' pony paths leading to collecting areas where stags are shot in the necessary autumn cull. Many of these paths follow old rights-of-way or obvious glen routes and there is nothing like a stretch of trackless glen (such as Gleann Gaorsaic!) to make one appreciate their presence.

BEN MORE, MULL

STARTING POINT
Teanga Brideig on A849 in Glen
More, 2 miles (3 km) up from Loch
Scridain. Parking on old road by
bridge (48-564306).
FINISHING POINT (OR START OF
NORTHERN ROUTE)
B8035 along Loch na Keal at the
Abhainn na h-Uamha. Roadside
parking (48-506367).
LENGTH
7 miles (11 km)
ASCENT
3600 ft (1100 m)

Ben More, Skye hills apart, is the highest peak in all the
Hebrides and so has a marvellously dominant lordship over the
western seaboard. However, don't rush to Mull to climb Ben
More only. Enjoy the island and, on some peerless morning,
head off up the big hill.

The island setting ensures that the hill is never busy, but it
does also occupy a special place for those climbing all the
Munros, frequently being kept as the celebratory 'last Munro'.
Ben More's tent-shaped crest is instantly recognized from many
view-points and it is a bold, rugged hill, giving a grand ascent in
keeping with the special nature of the delightful island of Mull.
There are also two Corbetts (the listed 2500 ft/762 m summits),
so Mull has big hills as well as many hills and offers a great
variety of ascents and through routes.

Ben More can be climbed by many different routes, the
quickest and easiest being from Dhiseig on Loch na Keal, but

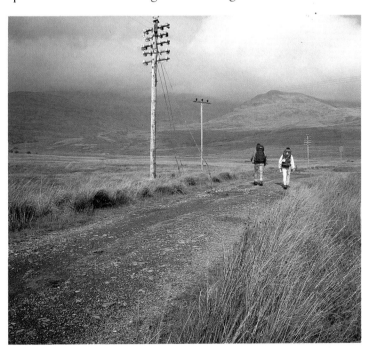

The old road through Glen More, Mull

ACCESS

A traverse of the mountain means a transport problem so there has to be a non-climbing driver willing to drop people off and collect them later, or you form two groups walking in opposite directions, or you have two cars. (The price of the ferry encourages you to cross with a full car!) As some such arrangement may not always be possible, alternative circuits, south and north, are also described. The main description is of a south–north traverse, from Glen More to Loch na Keal.

Glen More is really two east–west glens sharing a single name and clearly demarcating Ben More to the south. From Craignure there are 17 miles (27 km) of narrow road to the start. The road swings round (by new plantings) above a chain of lochs to pass a watershed and down into the western part of Glen More. At Craig, the only building in the glen, you have perhaps the finest local view of Ben More. As the glen levels out you reach Teanga Brideig, the starting-point.

This point is easily spotted, as there is a graceful wee bridge (with a guardian holly tree), part of the older motor road before realignments were made. Park on the old road, west of the burn.

Deer-stalking takes place from mid-August to near the end of October. An ascent of Ben More is seldom affected, but check locally (tel.: Aros (06803) 410). The Bartholomew 1:100,000 map, number 47, is useful as it covers the whole island and its approaches in one sheet.

such a fine peak deserves a worthy traverse, rather than the easiest option. Ben More or A' Chioch, above the 2000–2300 ft (600–700 m) level, is a mix of scree, rocks and boulders, so be adequately shod for such rough going.

ROUTE DESCRIPTION (Map 32)

There is a notice pointing out the route, an old right-of-way, still a clear path which can be seen curving up the first slopes, east of the two torrent gashes (1).

The Allt Teanga Brideig is 'stream of St Bride's tongue of land', Mull having as many saints as castles (2).

The path leads up to a distinctive col. The north side down into Glen Clachaig is much steeper. The old route descends it to Loch Ba and the head of Loch na Keal before crossing the 2-mile (3 km) neck of land to Salen, a fine alternative walk if Ben More refuses to clear of cloud. The col is not named (it is Mam Clachaig, 'pass of the stony route'), but the cairn is Carn Cul Righ Albainn ('cairn with its back on Scotland', traditionally a boundary mark between Picts and Scots).

Turn west up the ridge, which is simply followed to the top of A' Chioch (3). The R edge is the scalloped head of Glen Clachaig, so route-finding is not difficult. The summit is 'a great heap of rubble' or 'a crumbling ruin', depending on whom you read. A' Chioch (c. 2780 ft, c. 850 m) is 'the pap' and back, across the pass, Cruachan Dearg ('the red peak') is a similar symmetrical cone. The best of A' Chioch is the view to it from Ben More, so press on!

A brief bouldery descent leads to the splendid arc of ridge running to Ben More and bounded by the great northern corrie. This narrow crest calls for some scrambling but easy options are always available and it is possible to traverse below the crest on this south side if it is too intimidating or if a gale is blowing across the ridge. The scramble along the crest, however, is what makes this approach memorable. A last flourish (boulders again) leads to the summit Ordnance Survey obelisk on the stony plateau and a view which doubles in scale at a stride.

On a clear day the view can extend from Errigal in Ireland to Ben Nevis, and from the Hebrides to Galloway. Westwards lies the long arm of land known as the Ross of Mull. Off its extremity is Iona, the island of St Columba and the burial place of the early Scottish kings. The island of Erraid is also there, the scene of the shipwreck in R. L. Stevenson's masterpiece *Kidnapped*. The chunky island well out to sea is Staffa, which has Fingal's Cave, with its romantic musical and literary associa-

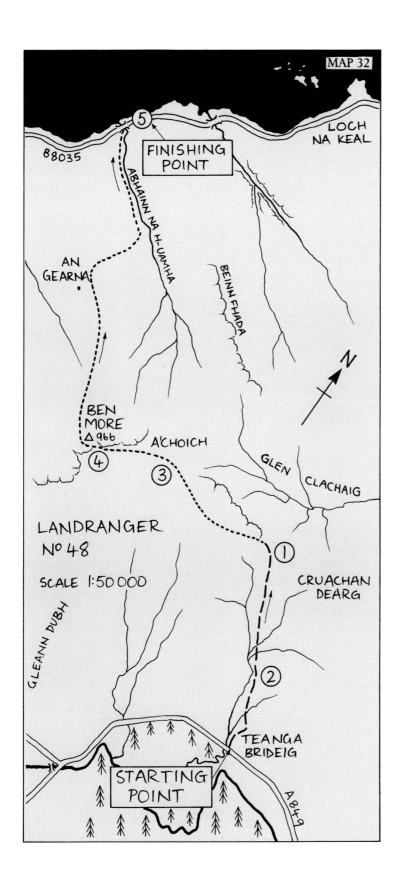

MAP 32

LOCH
NA KEAL

B8035

FINISHING
POINT

⑤

ABHAINN NA H-UAMHA

AN
GEARNA

BEINN FHADA

N

BEN
MORE
△ 966

A'CHOICH

④

③

GLEN
CLACHAIG

①

LANDRANGER
Nᵒ 48

CRUACHAN
DEARG

SCALE 1:50 000

GLEANN DUBH

②

TEANGA
BRIDEIG

STARTING
POINT

A849

tions. The Cuillin of Rhum and the Cuillin of Skye are arrayed behind the Ardnamurchan peninsula, the most westerly point of mainland Britain. Ulva and the Treshnish Islands lie at the mouth of Loch na Keal. On Mull you have landscape, seascape and cloudscape.

The compass can be completely erratic on top of Ben More *(4)*, so careful navigation is needed in cloud. The great bite of the northern corrie can hardly be missed, however, and following its edge gives help at the start of the descent. There are also cairns marking the route. By the time the dome of An Gearna (with a prominent cairn) is reached, you are usually out of cloud and can descend to Loch na Keal almost anywhere. Dhiseig farmhouse is the *voie normale* but my preference is to swing north-east to join the Abhainn na h-Uamha ('the river of the cave') for this has many fine pools and falls, the former very welcome on a hot day. Where stream meets road is also a clear rendezvous for a driver trying to link up with walkers. There is plenty of roadside parking *(5)*.

If you have to return to the start, the slaggy south ridge can be followed, bearing off to Maol nan Damh ('dome of the hind') and then down Coire nan Each ('horse corrie') and Gleann Dubh ('black glen') to cut round once the lower slopes are reached. Or descend due south to the charming Loch Beg. At low tide you can cross direct (by the marker posts) to the Kinloch Hotel on the south shore. Either way, an hour's walking takes you back to Teanga Brideig.

My recommended circuit from the north would be to wander up Gleann na Beinn Fhada to the col at its head and then ascend A' Chioch's north-east ridge, which will provide 'variety for mind and muscle'. Traverse to and descend Ben More as already described. The traverse of knobbly Beinn Fhada ('long hill'), with a secretive lochan below its summit, is another good start, giving the full circuit of the grander, northern side of Ben More, a round of about 8 miles (13 km) with an ascent of 4250 ft (1300 m).

1 Historic pass
This is the route of an historic drove road (Mull once exported 2000 head of cattle a year), and also the way travellers went before the road round the Gribun was opened up. The Gribun is quite the most exciting drive on Mull and in wild weather can be dramatic, with waves crashing beside the road and the falls blowing back over the rocky bluffs. The sea was the main highway in Mull in ancient times.

Loch Scridain from Am Binnein

2 St Bride

There were several saints called Bride (Brigid or Bridget), the most famous being St Brigid of Kildare. Her saint's day was 12 February and an old Mull proverb said 'On St Bride's day the adder comes out of the hill' (that is, from hibernation). Keep an eye open for these beautiful creatures.

3 Geology

Mull's geology is complex but A' Chioch and Ben More are basalt peaks, the eroded, glaciated remnants of a great centre of volcanic activity. At Burgh a fossilized tree stands mute witness to the overwhelming lava flows, once 6000 ft (1830 m) thick and, as Ben More, the most elevated Tertiary basalt in Britain. The columns of basalt at Fingal's Cave on Staffa are world famous. At the end of the Ross of Mull, granite rounds the landscape and Iona is of gneiss, some of the oldest rock in the world. Marble was long quarried on Iona.

4 Compass errors

Magnetic anomalies in the Highlands are mostly found in the west. Most people know of the Cuillin summits and crests being badly affected, but there are many other areas where the compass can lead you astray. The northern slopes of Ladhar Bheinn once led me a merry dance in thick cloud and Compass Hill on Canna gives a warning in its name. The deflection seldom lasts long once off summits and crests, but it is leaving those places that most demands navigational accuracy.

5 Loch na Keal

Sarah Murray, the pioneering guidebook writer, travelled extensively on Mull in 1800. Along Loch na Keal she described her riding problems: 'In ascending I was obliged to lie on the horse's neck, and in descending almost on his tail, but for all that I could not help gazing at the huge masses of rock piled like folio books one upon another, all the way up the mountain, hanging over my head.' When Lochbuie tried to keep her an extra day at Moy because of the wicked weather, she records that her servant expostulated 'In truth, sir, it can't hurt her, for the rain will only drive on her back.' The trees at the head of Loch na Keal have that rising, planed-off appearance that testifies to strong winds. As locals warn, 'Beware the westerly weather.' If the weather is hopeless, you can always retreat to the Mull Little Theatre and Restaurant at Dervaig.

A stream on Ben More

The Hidden Heart of Torridon

STARTING POINT
Car-park, off A896
Kinlochewe–Torridon road. OS
Outdoor Leisure Map 8 *The Cuillin and
Torridon Hills* (958568).
FINISHING POINT
Car-park, off minor road from
Torridon to Diabeg. OS Outdoor
Leisure Map 8 *The Cuillin and Torridon
Hills* (869576).
LENGTH
Glens only: 7½ miles (12 km).
Including Coire Mhic Fhearchair: 10
miles (16 km). Including Ruadh-stac
Mor: 12½ miles (20 km).
ASCENT
Glens only: 1020 ft (310 m). Including
Coire Mhic Fhearchair: 1700 ft (520
m). Including Ruadh-stac Mor: 3050
ft (930 m).

ACCESS

The walk round Liathach is entirely on National Trust for Scotland land, so there is no restriction on access. The path to Coire Mhic Fhearchair is generally free as well and nobody is going to be stalking on the crazy quartz disintegration of Ruadh-stac Mor. Keeping to the path would be appreciated as the land northwards is all deer forest. By the car-parks at the starting- and finishing-points, map boards give information on the area.

This walk goes into some of the most magnificently wild country in Britain and, apart from the ascent of Ruadh-stac Mor, is on paths, which are rough in places, often 'slaistery' and yielding a loneliness of atmosphere quite unknown in England and seldom equalled in Scotland. The walk round Liathach by itself, on a good day, would be two grades lower, the visit to Coire Mhic Fhearchair one grade lower, than the full expedition, which includes the second highest summit in the Torridon Mountains. Thus, while the optimum outing is described, the route has these easier options. 'Easy' is relative. No other path described in this book goes over a landscape so stripped to the naked bones of creation, no other hills offer such a shock of massive verticalities. This is a walk on the wild side.

Route Description (Maps 33, 34)

The car-park lies on the north side of the road just west of the Allt Choire Dhuibhe Mhoir and the path sets off from between car-park and burn. A notice at the car-park points out the 'corrie of the hundred hills' across the glen on the lower slopes of Sgurr Dubh ('black peak'). These moraine deposits stand out clearest in the horizontal light of dawn or dusk and much of your day will be spent wandering through such 'lumpy' country *(1)*.

At first the path follows the stream, then heads more steeply up the hillside, so there is soon a bird's-eye view down onto the glen. Lochain an Iasgair below, is popular with fishermen. The square building by it is a boathouse; the trim cottage beyond is the Ling Hut *(2)*. Right of Sgurr Dubh the conical hill is Sgorr an Lochain Uaine ('peak of the green loch'). Both these are worthy Corbetts and behind them lie Beinn Liath Mor ('big grey hill') and Sgorr Ruadh ('red peak'), which are Munros.

The path rises continually (you do not realize by how much

MAP NOTE

For this walk Outdoor Leisure Map 8 *The Cuillin and Torridon Hills* is recommended. The route wanders on and off *three* 1:50 000 Landranger sheets, which is not very practical, and the Outdoor Leisure 1:25 000 scale is welcomed for its greater detail of what is particularly demanding terrain.

Liathach from the Coire Dubh path

until descending it again) and slowly you are hemmed in by the great crags of Liathach's prow (L) and the screes and gullies of mighty Beinn Eighe (R). Just before the path crosses the burn there is a boulder on the R which has neatly split in two. Stepping stones cross the burn. Another sprawling monster of a hill now fills the view ahead: Beinn Dearg ('red hill'), which falls short of Munro status by less than 3 ft (1 m) *(3)*.

The watershed is rather indefinite, but the path suddenly wends downwards noticeably. Soon after, an overgrown, crescent-shaped lochan lies to the R (the path crosses its tiny outflow) and, level with the far end, there is a cairn at a split in the path. Ignore the path heading off R and in 20 yards (18 m) two more cairns appear, marking the branching-off of another cairned route, R, which is the one to take for Coire Mhic Fhearchair. (The first fork also heads there but follows a rougher line and really only grew to prominence recently, beaten out by people coming out from Coire Mhic Fhearchair who had lost the original path.)

If you are just walking round behind Liathach, continue on the L options. After a brief rise the way ahead suddenly becomes visible. There is a bigger lochan, L, and its outflow curves away round under Beinn Dearg with several more lochans visible: this is the start of the Abhainn Coire Mhic Nobuil, which you follow down to the road. The path deteriorates badly as it is no longer an old 'made' path but merely one tramped out by passing walkers. Beware the black muddy bits!

Continuing on the (second) path R for Coire Mhic Fhearchair, the route weaves in and out and up and down the moraine deposits. A jutting crest suddenly gives a grand opening-up of the view and is a good spot for a pause *(4)*. Through the gap, R of Beinn Dearg, two more hills bulk large in the wilderness: Beinn en Eoin ('hill of the bird', a Corbett) and Beinn a' Chearcaill ('hill of the hoop'). Our path continues to curve round the flank of Sail Mhor, Beinn Eighe's westernmost peak, in a rhythm-destroying mix of boulders, bog and brae. There are plenty of alternatives but all (eventually) are squeezed upwards between the cleft north prow of Sail Mhor ('the big heel') and the tumbling waters draining the corrie of corries. When you reach the loch, cross the outflow and wander round the other side for the best view.

Quite a few claim this to be the most spectacular corrie in the country *(5)* for it is built round by natural battlements and even the view outwards is to a landscape pared to primitive ferocity.

Descend from the corrie by the route of ascent and take the lower path options to return to the jutting crest described

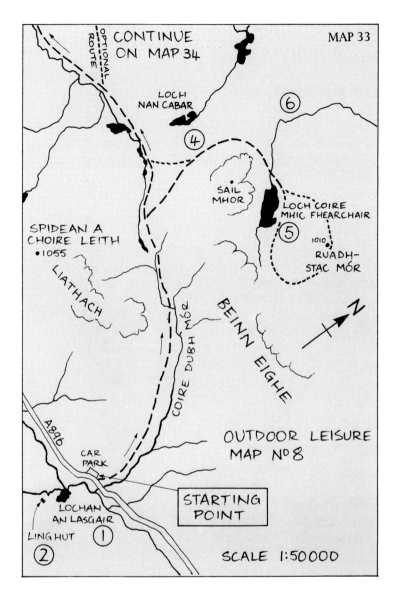

MAP 33

CONTINUE
ON MAP 34

OPTIONAL ROUTE

LOCH
NAN CABAR

④

⑥

SAIL
MHOR

LOCH COIRE
MHIC FHEARCHAIR

⑤

SPIDEAN A
CHOIRE LEITH
•1055

1010
RUADH-
STAC MÓR

LIATHACH

COIRE DUBH MÓR

BEINN EIGHE

N

OUTDOOR LEISURE
MAP N° 8

A896

CAR
PARK

STARTING
POINT

LOCHAN
AN LASGAIR

LING HUT ①

②

SCALE 1:50000

earlier, then head down (south-westwards) through the bumps towards the end lochan (Loch Grobaig) where the Coire Mhic Nobuil path is rejoined. Cutting the corner avoids the messy reaches along by the lochans.

The ascent of Ruadh-stac Mor ('big red peak') is probably enjoyed more in retrospect than during the ascent and descent, for the hill is a disintegrating mess of unfriendly quartzite, craggy or scree-girt and decidedly toilsome. Not for the timid or unfit. In ascent I find it simplest just to head a bit north of east and boldly ascend to the summit ridge, choosing a line with the minimum of scree. The summit is just the highest point of an elongated boulder plateau, which gives reasonable walking. With only Liathach higher, the toil is rewarded by a big view.

Meall a' Ghiubhais ('yew tree hill') is another Corbett, as is Ruadh-stac Beag, Beinn Eighe's next jutting arm to the east. Beinn Eighe is, aptly, 'hill of the file'. The wild country beyond Loch Maree lies to the north-west, the loch itself glimpsed down Glen Grudie *(6)*.

From the summit of Ruadh-stac Mor head along and down to the neck which links the Munro to the main body of Beinn Eighe, and turn down into Coire Mhic Fhearchair by a rubbishy gully which is easier to descend than to climb. The ground, lower, is *very* broken and rough, with crags, boulders, bogs and streams galore. There is no set path: you 'dree your own weird' as we say. The east side of the loch is easier, but the more adventurous may choose to pass round between loch and Sail Mhor. Contour back and cut down as described above.

Liathach ('the grey one') with its great corries, towers and ragged crests, is seen at its wildest and best from this side: a

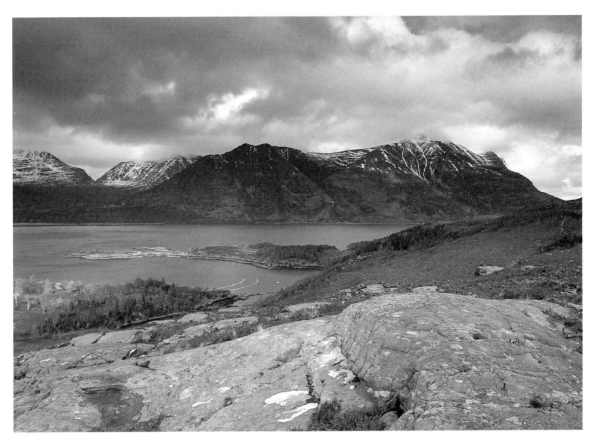

Liathach from above Shieldaig

mountaineer's mountain and one of the Top Ten in anybody's list of Scottish hills.

The walk down Coire Mhic Nobuil is no anti-climax for, ahead, looms Beinn Alligin, the third of the giants of Torridon and, above, Beinn Dearg takes on an ever-grander aspect. (Unlike Lot's Wife, you are urged to look back, often.) The path does improve when it becomes old, 'made' path again and eventually merges with the one descending from the Bealach Chomhla to the north and, shortly after, crosses a footbridge at the confluence of rivers. An excellent path takes you down the L bank to the road.

The river now cuts down into a gorge and in several places diversions to look at waterfalls are recommended: there are obvious paths and you can probably *hear* the falls. There is a pleasant one below the footbridge leading to Alligin *(7)* and one not far from the road, and the last is seen by looking over the parapet of the bridge when the road is reached. The last bit of path runs through old Scots pines *(8)* and the road twisting down to Loch Torridon is much enhanced by this forest remnant. The last mile (1.6 km) also gives views over the loch to yet more Torridonian peaks.

1 Geology

These moraine deposits which litter all the Torridon glens are relatively new, in a geological timescale, being the result of the last Ice Age, almost 10,000 years ago, not long before man appeared on the scene. The Torridon Hills, on the other hand, date back to the dawn of the world, fabulously contorted and fashioned by unbelievable forces. Liathach can glow pink from its sandstone massiveness, yet is capped by quartzite which, across the glen, lies at valley level. Early geologists were puzzled. They just could not envisage hills stood on end! Sgurr Dubh across the valley is a *grey* hill, largely made of this Cambrian quartzite. Our path, initially, is made of this stone, then becomes the warmer, rufous colour as we gain the Torridon sandstone.

2 Ling Hut

The Ling Hut of the Scottish Mountaineering Club is named after one of the great unsung heroes of early British climbing, Willie Ling. He roamed Scotland all his life and took part in endless first ascents both at home and abroad (often with Harold Raeburn) in places such as Norway, the Alps and the Caucasus.

3 Beinn Dearg

The ascent of Beinn Dearg is an alternative to visiting Coire Mhic Fhearchair and Ruadh-stac Mor. You are looking more or less along the route of ascent from here: a long, easy-rising ascent to the ridge and then various towers to bypass (not altogether straightforward) to reach the summit. Return by the same route unless carrying a parachute.

4 Fossils

Some of the quartz boulders on this knoll have good examples of fossilized worm casts. Just 20 yards (18 m) before you reach the knoll a big slab actually lies on the path.

5 The Great Corrie

The division between sandstone and quartzite can plainly be seen on the cliffs, the two strata separated by Broad Terrace—named by a climber and with some understate-ment. From the lip of the corrie your voice echoes round it.

6 Nature Reserve

Most of the Beinn Eighe is part of a National Nature Reserve, with an important remnant of old forest along the shores of Loch Maree—a habitat favoured by pine-martens, while, anywhere today, the lucky walker could spot a lazy golden eagle soaring overhead.

7 Great Cleft

This waterfall has the Great Cleft of Alligin as background. This huge rift in the mountain, leading from just below the summit, right down into the corrie, is the result of a gigantic rockfall. The fallen rocks are spread across the moor below the cliffs—a fascinating spot to explore. It is known as 'the foxes' corrie'.

8 *Regeneration*

In the hills, overgrazing by sheep and deer prevents any natural regeneration of trees, so it is only in inaccessible gorges such as this, that trees have survived: birch, rowan and holly among them.

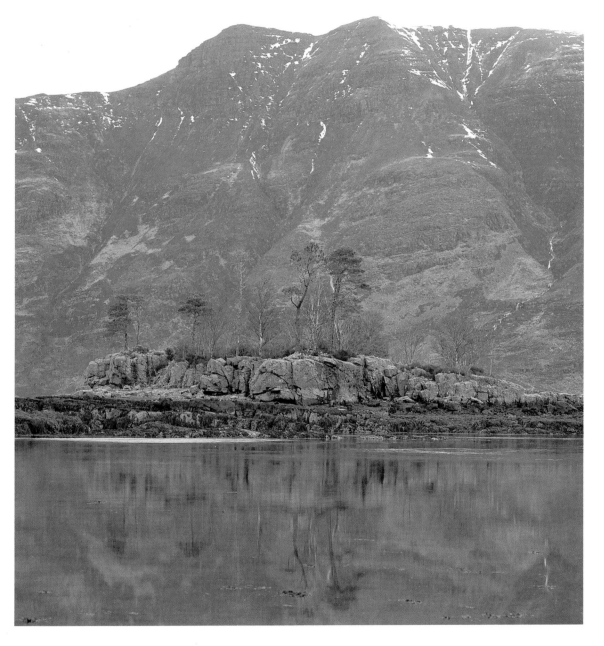

Liathach's western slopes above Loch Torridon

The Summits of Quinag

STARTING AND FINISHING
POINT
Car-park on the east side of A894 on
Lairig Unapool. (15-233274.)
LENGTH
8½ miles (14 km)
ASCENT
3940 ft (1200 m)

ACCESS
Access is straightforward from the
A894 Skiag Bridge – Unapool road.
There is a large off-road parking area
east of the road, at 233274, just ⅓
mile (500 m) short of the Lairig
Unapool watershed.

To drive from Ullapool to Unapool is to experience a sort of geological time warp. Startling hills crouch by the road like ambushing prehistoric monsters. Here are some of the oldest rocks in the world. In this skeleton of a place the protruding ribs of creation expose our puny human position of little and late. I have met people who have actually been frightened by the landscape of Coigach and Assynt. My own feelings never cease to be other than those of wonder—and surprise that a walker can venture into this vertical zoo relatively easily. Quinag, from most directions, looks as unapproachable as a panther but when you draw near you will hear the mountain purr.

ROUTE DESCRIPTION (Map 35)

Set off on the stalker's path almost opposite the car park, cross a burn and pull up for about ¼ mile (400 m) to gain a slight crest where you can swing L to gain the long westward-running ridge. It is well-defined with crags on its northern flank, and gives easy walking as the angle of ascent is the tilt of the quartzite strata which often breaks the surface, a surface which is completely littered with boulder debris. Despite the natural guidance of the edge, cairns have been erected. There is one rocky bump (15-212273), a small saddle, and then the final cone of the Corbett. The flat summit, from afar, looks like a well-defined castle but the main crags face north-east and one arrives quite unchallenged by difficulty. All the presumed difficulties will turn out to be imaginary but the setting is splendid and there is plenty of what climbers call 'exposure': the feeling of nothing below your boots! There is more green than expected and even if it is steep, there are few problems. When places are difficult they are obviously so.

The view is spread out as a grand panorama. Below is Loch Assynt and the big peaks of Inchnadamph backed by the Munros

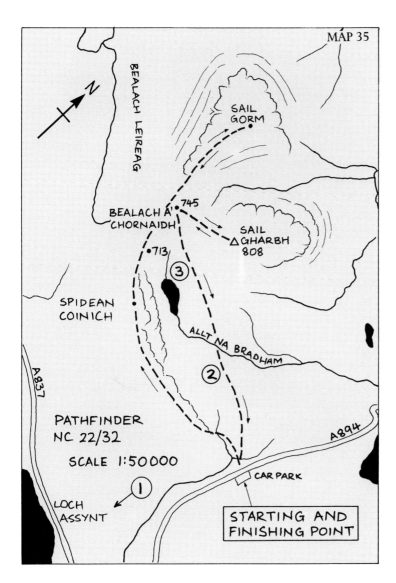

MAP 35

BEALACH LEIREAG

SAIL GORM

N

BEALACH A' CHORNAIDH

•745

SAIL GHARBH 808

•713

③

SPIDEAN COINICH

ALLT NA BRADHAM

②

A837

A894

PATHFINDER NC 22/32

SCALE 1:50000

①

CAR PARK

LOCH ASSYNT

STARTING AND FINISHING POINT

of Conival and Ben More; south is the grey Canisp and darker Suilven *(1)*; east are Glas Bheinn and Beinn Leoid among a huddle of hills; north is the cone of Ben Stack and the mass of Arkle; while running right down the west is a frieze of coastline with the arabesques of the Outer Hebrides beyond the glitter of the Minch. Marvellous.

We head off to the north-west, dropping to a level crest and then up to a bump of 2340 ft (713 m). Keep looking back, for the Spidean profile certainly calls for photographs. A steep path now twists down to the Bealach a' Chornaidh. Pause on the descent to look into the eastern corrie, for this will be the line of descent *(2)*.

A path now heads up the other side of the col (a rock band is turned on the right) to the 2450 ft (745 m) Centre Top, which

Quinag country

is really the hub of Quinag, from which spokes of ridge run out to the Corbetts. This is a good lunch spot and the day can always be shortened by missing out Sail Gorm and going directly to Sail Gharbh, the highest summit of Quinag.

Descend the north-west ridge if you are aiming for Sail Gorm. There is one flat-topped rock-banded bump to traverse (a look-alike to Spidean's 'castle') before the lowest point, then some minor swellings, with cliffs to the west, before a steady pull up to the eyrie-like summit. The corrie on the right is Bathaich Cuinneige, 'the barn of Quinag', and it is possible to follow its stream down to the coastal road, but this is untracked and a very demanding alternative. Golden eagles and ravens frequent this quiet corner.

You traverse back, unavoidably, to the Centre Top, then east to the dip on the broad ridge running up to Sail Gharbh, which has the only Ordnance Survey obelisk of the day. Sail Gharbh is, strictly speaking, the thrust of cliffs that terminates the ridge but, for convenience, is used for the summit as well; the same applies to Sail Gorm.

From the dip to Centre Top it is quite possible to drop down, on grass, to pick up the stalkers' path—a descent studied earlier in the walk. The cairned path keeps over from the loch but on a sun-smiting day a swim off its warm-coloured sand spit will call for a diversion. (I've seen deer paddling in its waters!) The path should be regained before it crosses the Allt na Bradhan as the ground beyond is very bouldery: sandstone boulders dug up and pushed down the hill by glacial action—like a dog digging in slow motion! *(3)* The path makes a pleasant end to a memorable walk.

1 *Suilven*
   This is a sort of Rock of Gibraltar set down in the Highlands. Norman McCaig, perhaps Scotland's finest living poet, has written many pieces about Suilven, his 'mountain of mountains'. Some are quoted in the anthologies *Speak to the Hills* and *Poems of the Scottish Hills* (Aberdeen University Press), and all appear in his *Collected Poems* (Chatto/Hogarth), one of the few such books to become a best-seller.

2 *Bealach a' Chornaidh path*
   The path on which you began the walk does not end as shown on the map. It continues roughly on the same line to the Allt na Bradhan, crosses the burn, then arcs up into the head of the corrie, keeping well away from and then above Lochan Bealach Cornaidh. A steep path also drops west from the Bealach to the Gleann Leireag path linking Loch Assynt and the coastal road. From that side Quinag appears as a long

craggy ridge, gully-riven and scree-skirted.

Water is largely absent from the crests but a traverse from the Bealach a' Chornaidh will usually find a trickle or, if you are desperate, the burn descending to the lochan can be visited without too much of a re-ascent. In places it runs underground: audible but unobtainable!

3 Geology

Quinag is largely made of Torridonian sandstone, part of the band running from Applecross to Cape Wrath and including such great peaks as Liathach and An Teallach. Such was the earth's warping in the cataclysmic past that the underlying gneiss sometimes rises to some height—more than 1970 ft (600 m) on the prow of Sail Gorm. The highest cone of Quinag is actually a quartzite capping, a continuation of that so widely exposed on the ascent to Spidean Coinich and its 'castle'. Sail Gharbh's prow is of Torridonian sandstone, and as early as 1907, Raeburn, Ling and Mackay climbed its Barrel Buttress.

Ardvreck Castle, Loch Assynt

INTRODUCING THE CUILLIN OF SKYE

STARTING POINT
Sligachan, at the junction of the A850 and A863. Parking at or near the inn. OS Outdoor Leisure Map 8 *The Cuillin and Torridon Hills* (486298).

FINISHING POINT
Glenbrittle, where the path meets the glen road (424258) (or at bridge (416245) or elsewhere in the glen). OS Outdoor Leisure Map 8 *The Cuillin and Torridon Hills*.

LENGTH
Pass only: 4 miles (6.5 km)
Pass and Bruach na Frithe: 8 miles (13 km)

ASCENT
Pass only: 1190 ft (360 m)
Pass and Bruach na Frithe: 3350 ft (1020 m)

The Cuillin hills are unquestionably the wildest and most demanding range in Britain. Walkers often give the Cuillin a miss, believing them to be the preserve of the rock climber, but there are quite a few summits and passes which can be gained without technical difficulty. The following route, the Bealach a' Mhaim, is an ancient approach to remote Glenbrittle, having been used for centuries before the devious motor road was constructed. And with one of the easy Cuillin summits, Bruach na Frithe, lying above the pass, there is the bonus of a first scramble to the Cuillin crests. If you make that, then you are probably risking a lifetime of Cuillin exploration. If circumstances dictate a return to Sligachan (for the car, for instance) then reaching the pass and climbing Bruach na Frithe make for a grand day.

The Cuillin range from Elgol

ACCESS

Buses run from Armadale and Kyleakin to Broadford and Portree, passing Sligachan, the start of the walk. If you drive to Glenbrittle, let one person drive round to the finish and the rest of the party can follow this traditional approach to the glen.

SAFETY NOTE

This route includes what is probably the roughest ascent described in the book, so walkers should be well-shod and carry good waterproofs and essential food. The pass could be forced in most conditions, but the ascent of Bruach na Frithe is best kept for a clear day as it may be a grade above your past walking experience. Furthermore, the compass is unreliable on top, the ordinary map is inadequate, and such a major ascent deserves the reward of the spectacular view— one of the best in Britain. Parts of the route can be wet and boggy and, on the hill itself, you are scrambling on bare rock. If you have traversed Crib Goch or Striding Edge then you may be relieved to know the traverse of Bruach na Frithe is no harder.

*If you are heading for Bruach na Frithe, simply break off the main path to head up into the corrie.

BRUACH NA FRITHE

There are a variety of routes, so you can choose your own combination of ascent and descent lines.

Continued overleaf

ROUTE DESCRIPTION (Maps 36, 37)

There are many paths heading off over the moors from Sligachan, so some care is needed at the start. Sligachan itself *(1)* is in a fine setting, with the pachydermatous hulk of Glamaig above *(2)*, a fine old pack bridge with a view up Glen Sligachan to Marsco *(3)*, and the jagged crests of the Sgurr nan Gillean-Am Bastier end of the Cuillin breaking over the horizon like a rush of black waves. The view has enthralled generations of walkers and climbers.

The A850 Kyleakin–Portree road has a branch, the A863, turning off at Sligachan, this latter road heading on to Dunvegan, with a road off the road reaching Glenbrittle. There is plenty of parking space at or near the hotel. A realigned bit of road behind the hotel, off the A863, is useful. Walk up the sweeping curve of the A863 and just beyond a shallow cutting a small road, roughly-tarred and with grass along the middle, heads L onto the moor. A small sign indicates 'Footpath to Glenbrittle' and two lines of power and telephone poles also head off onto the moor. There is a small roadside car-park. Other tracks between the hotel and here should be ignored.

Follow this minor road. Its reason soon becomes obvious: road and posts head to a lonely, white building: Alltdearg House. At the gate pillar of its fenced-off grounds, turn R (an arrow is painted on the post) for a squelchy diversion before rejoining the old made path *(4)*.

The going is actually not too bad as the path winds up along beside the waters of the Allt Dearg Mor, a quite delightful burn with seemingly countless cascades and tempting pools. The jagged towers of Sgurr nan Gillean's Pinnacle Ridge stand out finely from the path with the blunt upthrust of Am Bastier and the battle-axe of the Bastier Tooth.

The Allt Dearg Mor gathers most of its waters in Coire na Circe, from which the path climbs up towards the Bealach a' Mhaim. As you look south, the big Fionn Choire is clear.* A spring, Tobar nan Uaislean *(5)* lies by the path on the last stretch to the pass *(6)*.

There is a pool on the watershed, marking the start of the Allt a' Mhaim. Then there is a proper lochan, beyond which a side path breaks off L to circle the head of Coire na Creiche, giving access to various climbs and a tricky pass to Coruisk. Continue on past a big cairn for the descent down into Glenbrittle. The size of the cairn is an indication of the long use of this pass. The path angles down for ⅝ mile (1 km) to the corner of the huge forestry plantations which you skirt until you reach the motor road to Glenbrittle.

ASCENT 1

A cairned path breaks off the main path from Coire na Circe and heads up west of the Allt an Fhionn-Choire to gain the ridge that demarcates the corrie on its west side. Once the crest of this North-west Ridge is gained it is just a matter of picking a line along and up it to the summit. In places there is some scrambling but any trickier places can be bypassed on the R or L flanks. Keep to the crest as much as possible or you may traverse off onto real crags. Climbers would regard this as an easy ridge but walkers who normally amble hands-in-pockets will find it a novel excitement. *(9)*

ASCENT 2

The completely easy way is simply to wander up the Fionn Choire, a surprisingly green and flowery place as the surface is somewhat porous (even the streams vanish in places), to reach the scree-covered slopes at the head of the corrie. Climb up to the lowest point on the ridge and ascend the easy East Ridge. Bruach na Frithe is topped by the Main Ridge's only Ordnance Survey obelisk. Most of this route is cairned or well-worn in the upper parts.

ALTERNATIVE DESCENTS

The East Ridge and Fionn Choire provide the easiest way down from Bruach na Frithe, but the North-west Ridge is the most entertaining and can be followed all the way down to the saddle of the Bealach a' Mhaim. Heed the warnings about navigational problems in cloud—and keep this hill for a clear day. All running water from the Fionn Choire ends at Sligachan, so you should be mislaid rather than lost.

Opposite: The classic view to the Cuillin from Sligachan

There is a good view into Coire na Creiche, a huge empty bowl drained by the River Brittle, another river with many waterfalls *(7)*. The other side of the corrie is dominated by the prow of Sgurr Thuilm and jutting out from the back of the corrie is the split triangular peak of Sgurr an Fheadain.

From the point where you reach the road it is 2¼ miles (3.5 km) to the hostel, 2¾ miles (4.5 km) to the hut and other houses, and 3½ miles (5.5 km) to the campsite. If being met by a car, the bridge over the River Brittle, ⅝ mile (1 km) down the valley, is a good rendezvous (8-416245).

1 Sligachan

The historic inn here was the base for much of the early exploration of the Cuillin. The visitors' book dating back to those days has, alas, been stolen and something of the atmosphere has gone as busloads of trippers swarm around in the summer. It was to the inn that the great Norman Collie retired in the lonely war years. Richard Hillary in his classic story of his flying days, *The Last Enemy*, paints a picture of Collie, and their own escapade on the Sligachan hills. C. Mill's *Norman Collie, A Life in Two Worlds* (Aberdeen University Press) is a recent biography I can recommend.

2 Glamaig

This brutal Corbett was the scene of an early escapade which still offers a feat hard to emulate. In 1899 one of General Bruce's Gurkhas romped up and down Glamaig, in bare feet, in just 55 minutes. In 1955 George Rhodes took a couple of minutes longer, but I have not read of any improvement on the time.

3 Marsco

This is the hill that dominates the view up Glen Sligachan even if it does not make Corbett height. A traverse from Glamaig to Marsco is one of Skye's great walks as it gives an endless view to the Black Cuillin. These hills are Red Cuillin and largely composed of crumbling red granite screes, so careful route-finding is called for. Glen Sligachan offers a long walk through to Loch Scavaig or Elgol. One renowned hiker through Glen Sligachan was Bonnie Prince Charlie during his wanderings after Culloden. Obviously conditions have changed little. An old lady, dealing with his feet after the walk, commented 'Filthy lad!'

4 Weather

To be fair, a warning should be given about Skye's weather. The siting of such big hills in the west ensures that they receive a large share of our moist westerly weather. Wet here can be very wet indeed and in prolonged rain one should simply flee, and come again. There is a tremendous run-off of

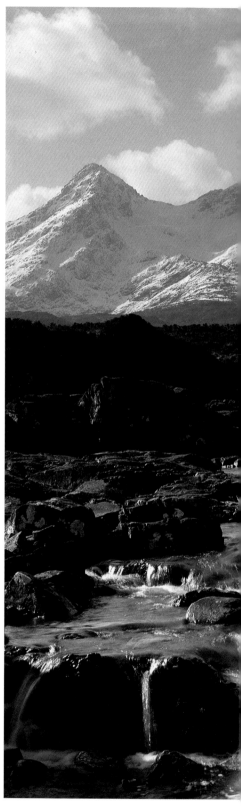

water and in a heatwave the Cuillin can be surprisingly waterless. The moors round the hills, often lying on impervious rock, act as sponges and the paths across them have become black morasses.

5 *Tobar nan Uaislean*

'The well of the gentlemen' is a well in the Scottish sense; that is, a spring. It lies just below the path a couple of minutes short of the watershed.

6 *The Bealach a' Mhaim*

'The pass of the rounded hill' is usually just called the Mam ('the saddle'), which is what it is rather than a defile. If you are not contemplating the ascent of Bruach na Frithe, then wander up onto Am Ban above, to enjoy the panoramic view, which is obscured in the pass itself.

7 *Coire na Creiche*

This is 'the corrie of the spoils', 'spoils' referring to rustled cattle. No doubt animals driven over the Bealach a' Mhaim were secreted here successfully. No road entered the glen in those days. A vicious clan battle here saw the MacDonalds defeat the MacLeods in 1601, a fray which much embarrassed James VI, who was trying to impress Queen Elizabeth I of England with his control of Scotland.

The Cuillin was once the centre of violent volcanic activity. A slow-cooking lava formed the rough, dark gabbro rock we all love. Basalt intrusions have eroded more rapidly and have created the gullies and chimneys which are so characteristic. Waterpipe Gully, down Sgurr an Fheadain, is

The Allt Dearg Mor with the Gillean–Am Basteir hills beyond

169

typical. Finally, it was the scouring glaciers that dug out the corries and left the narrow crests. The geology of Skye is very much open to the eye.

Coire na Creiche is one of only five sites (all in Skye) where the alpine rock cress *Arabis alpina* grows in Britain. The gabbro does not produce an exciting flora but you will meet all the alpine regulars. And in a few places there are special plants like the above.

8 *The road to Glenbrittle*

About 5 miles (8 km) from Sligachan you leave the Dunvegan road to take a side road for Carbost and 1¼ miles (2 km) later this is in turn left for a narrow road over desolate moors. There are grand views of the Cuillin as the road dips through the plantings.

9 *Bruach na Frithe*

Bruach na Frithe (pronounced *Broo-ach na Free*), 'slope of the deer forest', is 3143 ft (958 m) and will probably have taken 3–4 hours to scale, from Sligachan. The first recorded ascent was made in May 1845 by Professor Forbes, the early glaciologist, who dutifully took his barometer to the top.

Beyond the jagged crest over Am Basteir looms Sgurr nan Gillean (3166 ft, 965 m), 'the peak of the young men'. At Bruach na Frithe the Main Ridge turns sharply southwards over the least-visited lower section before the complex peaks of Sgurr a' Mhadaidh and Sgurr a' Ghreadaidh lead on to the most popular area above Glenbrittle. This area includes Sgurr Alasdair (3257 ft, 993 m), Skye's highest peak, the Inaccessible Pinnacle, the most difficult of all Munros, and Sgurr na Banachdich, the only other walkers' Munro in the Cuillin. A traverse of the whole ridge is still regarded as one of the greatest days possible on our hills.

Skye winter: the right skyline ridge leads from the pass up to Bruach na Frithe

Appendices

Access

It is frequently said that there is no law of trespass in Scotland, but that statement is erroneous. The modern situation is that walkers and climbers have a factual freedom-to-roam in wild places provided there is consideration for estate needs, and that countryside sensibilities operate.

It is because of this *de facto* situation that there is widespread public misunderstanding about the *de jure* position. The law says that a landowner has the right to request a walker to leave his land, and may possibly exert just sufficient force to achieve that object; a situation fraught with the possibility of counter-charges, and which rarely happens and which, in many cases in Scotland, would not be obeyed. The mere fact of being on the ground in Scotland is not, *of itself*, an offence and legal actions over access are a matter of the civil, not the criminal, law.

Such actions over access are virtually unheard of, and most Scottish walkers passionately believe they have a *moral* right to wander in wild places and will not surrender it. However, such an attitude should be accompanied by a knowledge of estate and farming needs. In outlining the legal position, one must emphasize that the main feature of walker–landowner relationships in Scotland is one of cordial co-existence on a voluntary basis.

Traditional freedom to roam in Scotland was greatly changed by nineteenth-century legislation that resulted from the creation of the big sporting estates, and which enabled owners to take prohibitive legal action against people walking on their ground. Some routes were obviously needed for community purposes such as droving, funerals, ways to markets, or passage between settled communities, and corridor rights-of-way were then defined which had the protection of the law,

and which still exist as legal, free-access routes. There were some spectacular court cases before these routes were clarified.

As the years passed and the social pattern of ownership of hill areas changed, and as more and more people went to the outdoors, this situation eased. Men who took part in two world wars were in no mood for restrictions on walking when they returned. And as the outdoor boom developed, a *de facto* freedom-to-roam evolved.

A landowner can still take legal, civil action against a walker to prevent him entering or re-entering the ground, but normally has to prove damage or harm before such a ban would be granted by the court. As no damage is normally caused by walking hills, glens and moors, examples of such litigation are very few.

The Trespass (Scotland) Act 1865 means the police can be involved if fires are lit without permission or camping is carried out without permission. This legislation was originally brought in to deal with the travelling people, the tinkers, camping on sites against the wishes of the owner. It has been used against hillwalkers in modern times in some isolated instances.

Scotland now has a situation whereby most landowners recognize the desire of people to walk and make no attempt to prevent it, but understandably seek co-operation over deer stalking dates and at some other key times. Most walkers believe freedom to roam in the hills to be a moral right and will not surrender it, but want to cause no bother. Privacy, crops, farm stock and agricultural needs must be respected. Reservoirs and park land are covered by regulations. The extent and range of relatively wild land in Scotland and a small population of five million help this situation to work although there are some localized pressure-points.

Modern factors which can affect freedom to roam include the growth of private forestry plantations, which can blanket some access glens or paths, the Ministry of Defence closing certain areas; or new owners who do not understand Scottish traditions; or the behaviour of some cavalier walkers.

DOGS
Where there are sheep around, dogs are best kept on a leash. They can be shot on sight if a shepherd has reasonable grounds for thinking sheep have been chased or frightened. Dogs should be under control at all times.

GATES
They must be shut after you unless they are already open when you get there, in which case they should be left open.

SHEEP
When sheep have lambs give them a wide berth in case you disturb ewes with sick young ones. If a lamb follows you, ignore it. If you see a shepherd or dogs driving sheep near you, get out of the way or sit still until they have passed.

LITTER
All litter should be taken home. Some countryside litter bins are anything but effective. They often have no lids, so scavengers spread the rubbish around and the wind scatters the top layers of paper and plastic.

GROUSE
The season starts on 12 August and has its peak during that month. It ends on 10 December. Such areas are easily recognized by the presence of shooting butts, small palisades or bunkers of stone, turf, wood or corrugated iron. Stay clear in season.

RED DEER
The stag shooting season runs from 1 July to 20 October, and that for hinds from 21 October to 15 February. In practice, the main time is mid-August to round mid-October. Few estates request walkers to stay off the hills from July to February and those who do are a bone of contention. Consult locally during the peak period or go to non-shooting hills, such as National Trust for Scotland ground. The balance between consultation on a route during shooting times and asking permission is a fine one, but the line should be recognized. Shooting is not traditionally carried out on a Sunday, but there are some modern exceptions to this and walkers can move the deer on a Sunday to the detriment of an estate plan for the Monday. The letting of shooting rights or the sale of venison form a major part of the income of many estates.

In outlining the legal position and countryside behaviour in Scotland, one must make it clear that the overall position is currently a relatively happy one. A series of legal actions would end current co-existence and could not be made to stick, and landowners would be the ultimate losers. Uncaring and irresponsible individual climbers and walkers can do untold harm. No one wants friction and that is how it should be. Freedom-to-roam is a precious heritage, but it brings responsibilities for caring behaviour with it and many walkers are glad to number estate owners, factors, shepherds and stalkers among their close friends, and vice versa.

Safety

The wildness and remoteness of parts of Scotland, especially the Highlands, cannot be emphasized too strongly. For those used to walking in England, there is an altogether different, harder challenge, both mentally and physically. In the Lake District, for example, you are seldom more than a few miles from a road—and Lakeland would fit into Rannoch Moor nicely. In the Highlands, however, there are some sheets of the 1:50 000 map with only a few inches of red road marked on them. The walking game is a far more serious one in the north.

Even some of the easy walks can be hazardous at times. You should think twice before a Caithness clifftop walk when a gale is raging through the Pentland Firth, and parts of the Borders can be very remote from any help in an emergency. The rather parrot-fashion rules need to be supplanted by a single, vital imperative: THINK. The hills can get round the rules, having plenty of original dirty tricks for the unwary but, whatever the circumstances, there is always a best action/reaction. Don't panic. Think the situation through and do your best. A few basic guidelines may help.

Go well equipped. An efficient waterproof, windproof 'shell' and adequate warm layers underneath should be the norm. A 'bivvy' bag should be carried.

Make sure you have map and compass, and know how to use them. All the party should be able to navigate, not just the leader.

If going alone, leave some indication of your plans. Walking alone is a valid mountain game, not lightly undertaken however, and best learnt on easy terrain. The harder walks in this book are only suitable for the experienced solo walker.

Be prepared to modify routes when weather or circumstances dictate; as many accidents are caused by sticking to a set plan as by neglecting one. The hills have the last say, not us.

Carry useful foods, and some extra. The calories will be burnt up at a great rate and need to be replaced: little and often is sound advice. Take in plenty of liquid. A group can carry a pan and stove and enjoy brewing-up. You watch your car's fuel gauge, so watch your own consumption.

Keep an eye on the weather. Ask local advice or make use of TV or radio forecasts. Obtain, and use, a Met Office card listing telephone numbers for area forecasts.

Carry a basic first aid kit. Deal with any rubbing on heels at once; blisters not only cripple, they cause delays and benightments. Learn some first aid; it could save a life. If there is an accident, keep calm. Render such first aid as you can and shelter the patient. Write down a six-figure grid reference and a note of the injuries. *Then* head out for help. The nearest telephone may be nearly a day's walk away, remember. Dial 999 and pass on the information to the police, who organize rescue services in Scotland.

Be comfortable in your walking. Wear appropriate clothing and footwear for the weather and conditions. Take off and put on garments as required. Often the summit is not the best place to rest. Find better shelter and keep warm. Conversely, avoid overheating. Heat exhaustion is not uncommon. Wearing waterproofs in a heatwave is not a good idea, but it is seen and, in one case, heat exhaustion was put down to hypothermia because the symptoms seem the same. There is no substitute for thinking, so

THINK
THINK
THINK.

Giving a Grid Reference

Giving a grid reference is an excellent way of 'pinpointing' a feature, such as a church or mountain summit, on an Ordnance Survey map.

Grid lines, which are used for this purpose, are shown on the 1:25 000 Outdoor Leisure, 1:25 000 Pathfinder and 1:50 000 Landranger maps produced by the Ordnance Survey; these are the maps most commonly used by walkers. Grid lines are the thin blue lines one kilometre apart going vertically and horizontally across the map producing a network of small squares. Each line, whether vertical or horizontal, is given a number from 00 to 99, with the sequence repeating itself every 100 lines. The 00 lines are slightly thicker than the others thus producing large squares each side representing 100 km and made up of 100 small squares. Each of these large squares is identified by two letters. The entire network of lines covering the British Isles, excluding Ireland, is called the National Grid.

FIGURE 3 *Giving a grid reference*

The left-hand diagram above shows a corner of an Ordnance Survey 1:50 000 Landranger map which contains a Youth Hostel. Using this map, the method of determining a grid reference is as follows:

Step 1

Holding the map in the normal upright position, note the number of the 'vertical' grid line to the left of the hostel. This is 72.

Step 2

Now imagine that the space between this grid line and the adjacent one to the right of the hostel is divided into ten equal divisions (the right-hand diagram does this for you). Estimate the number of these 'tenths' that the hostel lies to the right of the left-hand grid line. This is 8. Add this to the number found in Step 1 to make 728.

Step 3

Note the number of the grid line below the hostel and add it on to the number obtained above. This is 21, so that the number becomes 72821.

Step 4

Repeat Step 2 for the space containing the hostel, but now in a vertical direction. The final number to be added is 5, making 728215. This is called a six-figure grid reference. This, coupled with the number or name of the appropriate Landranger or Outdoor Leisure map, will enable the Youth Hostel to be found.

A full grid reference will also include the identification of the appropriate 100 kilometre square of the National Grid; for example, SD 728215. This information is given in the margin of each map.

Addresses of Useful Organizations

Association for the Protection of
Rural Scotland,
14a Napier Road,
Edinburgh, EH10 5AY.
Edinburgh (031) 229 1081

Central Scotland Countryside Trust
Heron House, Wellside Place,
Falkirk,
Central, FK1 5SE.
Falkirk (0324) 37598

Conservation Bureau,
Scottish Development Agency,
Rosebery House,
Haymarket Terrace,
Edinburgh, EH12 5EZ.
Edinburgh (031) 337 9595

Countryside Commission for Scotland,
Battleby,
Redgorton,
Perth, PH1 3EW.
(0738) 27921

Forestry Commission,
Public Information Division,
231 Corstorphine Road,
Edinburgh, EH12 7AT.
Edinburgh (031) 334 0303

Mountaineering Council for Scotland,
4E Battery Terrace,
Oban,
Argyll, PA34 5DN.

National Trust for Scotland,
5 Charlotte Square,
Edinburgh, EH2 4DU.
Edinburgh (031) 226 5922

Orkney Heritage Society,
48 Junction Road,
Kirkwall,
Orkney.
Kirkwall (0856) 2632

Scottish Conservation Projects Trust,
Balallan House,
24 Allan Park,
Stirling,
Central, FK8 2QG.
Stirling (0786) 79697

Scottish Countryside Activities Council,
39 Clepington Road,
Dundee, DD4 7EL.
Dundee (0382) 41095

Scottish Countryside Rangers Group,
c/o Lochore Meadows Country Park,
Crosshill,
Lochgelly,
Fife, KY5 8BA.
Lochgelly (0592) 860086

Scottish Inland Waterways Association,
139 Old Dalkeith Road,
Edinburgh, EH16 4SZ.
Edinburgh (031) 664 1070

Scottish Recreational Land Association,
18 Abercromby Place,
Edinburgh, EH3 6TY.
Edinburgh (031) 556 4466

Scottish Rights of Way Society,
1 Lutton Place,
Edinburgh, EH8 9PD.
Edinburgh (031) 447 9242

Scottish Tourist Board,
23 Ravelston Terrace,
Edinburgh, EH4 3EU.
Edinburgh (031) 332 2433

Scottish Youth Hostels Association,
7 Glebe Crescent,
Stirling,
Central, FK8 2JA.
Stirling (0786) 51181

Scottish Wildlife Trust,
25 Johnston Terrace,
Edinburgh, EH1 2NH.
Edinburgh (031) 226 4602

INDEX

Page numbers in *italics* refer to illustrations.